The Expansion and Transformations
of Courtly Literature

MS fr. 119, fol. 312v   Phot. Bibl. Nat. Paris

THE EXPANSION AND TRANSFORMATIONS OF COURTLY LITERATURE

EDITED BY

NATHANIEL B. SMITH

AND

JOSEPH T. SNOW

THE UNIVERSITY OF GEORGIA PRESS
ATHENS

This volume is composed of selected papers from the Second Triennial Congress of the International Courtly Literature Society.

Copyright © 1980 by the University of Georgia Press
Athens 30602

Set in 11 on 14 point Mergenthaler Bembo type
Printed in the United States of America

Library of Congress Cataloging in Publication Data

Main entry under title:
The Expansion and transformations of courtly literature.

1. Literature, Medieval—History and criticism—Addresses, essays, lectures. 2. Courtly love—Addresses, essays, lectures. I. Smith, Nathaniel B. II. Snow, Joseph T.
PN682.C6E9   809'.933'54   79-10053
ISBN 0-8203-0476-X

William Calin's article, "Defense and Illustration of *Fin' Amor*: Some Polemical Comments on the Robertsonian Approach," first appeared in the fall 1978 issue of the *Stanford French Review*. The permission of the editor to reprint the material here is gratefully acknowledged.

In Memoriam
Eugène Vinaver
1899–1979

Contents

V. A Concluding Proposal

Editorial Consultants

Preface

With the belief that an overall theme would provide a coherent and interdisciplinary investiga-
tive effort worthy of an international gathering
held but once every three years, we asked potential participants to orient their contributions toward
aspects of "the expansion and transformations of courtly
literature." Ultimately the theme would not only give the
Second Triennial Congress of the International Courtly
Literature Society a focal point but also be the keystone of
a volume of selected papers tracing not so much the genesis as the ulterior development of what is beyond doubt
the central phenomenon marking medieval vernacular
literature.

Twelve papers have been selected from among the 127
presented in the 41 sections exploring, from a great variety
of perspectives, the evolution of courtly literature. Two
of the plenary addresses, those of Eugène Vinaver and
William Melczer, frame the ten other papers ranging
from twelfth-century France and Germany to the Scottish
Renaissance.

Professor Vinaver regrettably was prevented by illness
from attending; however, he contributed his inspiration
not only through his paper, read by Barry Gaines as the
closing act of the Congress, but also through the common
training, reminiscences, and reading of papers by so many
of his former students, colleagues, and admirers. May the
present volume, which attests the Vinaver heritage in seen

and unseen ways, help perpetuate this great scholar's humane and humanistic approach to the courtly world.

This volume represents the good will and hard work, the ideas and dedicated service, of many others. We would like to thank the officers and members of ICLS, without whom the Second Congress could never have been so fruitful a gathering; the editorial consultants who aided in selecting papers and made many valuable suggestions; and the authors who willingly revised their papers for written presentation.

Our gratitude also goes to John Stephens, former dean of the Franklin College of Arts and Sciences of the University of Georgia, and to the Department of Romance Languages and the Medieval Studies Program, for the financial support which helped make it possible to bring the Congress to Athens. Our colleagues on the Local Planning Committee—Joseph Berrigan, Mia Cocco, Freeman Henry, William Provost, Jim Ward, and Victoria Thomas—gave very generously of their time to ensure the smooth running of the diverse activities of the Congress. Suzanne Lindenau supervised the recording of selected highlights of several meetings and has made tapes available at cost to congressants through the University of Georgia Language Laboratory. We are grateful to Raymond J. Cormier, Susanna Peters Coy, Alan Deyermond, and Lewis A. M. Sumberg for making suggestions on the first draft of our introduction, and to Martha Smith for preparing the index. Finally, we wish to express deep appreciation to Marcie Copenhaver for all that her unerring typing skills have contributed.

N.B.S.
J.T.S.

Introduction

Courtly Love and Courtly Literature

NATHANIEL B. SMITH AND JOSEPH T. SNOW

he coining of the expressions *courtly love* and *courtly literature* has caused nothing but trouble. Yet trouble, in the etymological sense of turbulence, keeps scholarship vigorous and stimulates a flow of rich new ideas. Even if scholars have not yet succeeded in defining to everyone's satisfaction what courtly literature really is, perhaps we can comfort ourselves that the founding, some five years ago, of the International Courtly Literature Society and this society's continued growth, in themselves, contribute substantially to the open exchange and evolution of ideas. The First Triennial Congress of the ICLS (Philadelphia, 1974) and the Second Triennial Congress (Athens, Georgia, 1977), brought into contact many distinguished scholars; now, the moment seems right for a publication intended to explore and consolidate current efforts in these areas.

The past decade has seen a number of collaborative volumes or journal issues devoted to medieval literature.[1] And in these, a central concern has inevitably been the *querelle de l'amour courtois*. It was placed in bold relief and given new directions by the 1967 Binghamton conference and the long and important reviews of its published proceedings.[2] The time has not yet come for the defenders or the equally valiant assailants of the castle of courtly love to retire from the fray; the battle is still joined, and in fact victory for one side or the other might be a double defeat. Tension and paradox inform today's scholarly skirmishes much as they shaped the poetry and prose of the medieval writers who first gave life and meaning to *fin' amor*.

Far from raising further controversy concerning the already battle-worn term *amour courtois*, the present volume hopes to create a strategic diversion by attracting critical attention toward the broader—and perhaps fairer—field of courtly *literature*. The blazon of courtly literature, like that of courtly love, is multihued and capable of subtle shapeshifting. Contributors have not been encouraged to adopt any common stance, for many of the terms we must deal with have a fluctuating meaning which, at any given time, depends on what most people take them to mean. Almost certainly Gaston Paris would have disagreed with sundry modern applications of what he first defined as *amour courtois*. But is this not proof of a living semantic evolution rather than cause for discarding the term entirely?

One could, of course, while remaining in good company, speak of *fin' amor*, or of *amour troubadouresque*, or of *amour chevaleresque*, or of "noble love," or of "medieval love,"[3] or (to be unimpeachably concrete) of Lancelotian love, or, as Terence Scully suggests (in n. 7 to his article), of *joie courtoise*. Still, if "for medieval writers, courtly love is real,"[4] for modern scholars the term itself is real, for better or worse—and real for its adversaries as well as its defenders, since to attack even an undefinable term is to come to grips with its existence.

The proper subject of literary criticism and literary history is literature not society, and the reality with which this volume deals is, at the very least, literary. Troubadours and trouvères did argue in verse the relative virtues of conjugal and extramarital love as well as that suitable to clerics and knights; not a few of them claimed to be the most perfect *entendedor* or *drut* of the single most worthy *domna*; the Tristan saga did, with time, become suffused with an amorous etiquette distinctly foreign to its origins. For all this and much more there is abundant textual proof. Courtly love and courtly literature, like individual manuscripts, thus become indubitable medieval artifacts. Whatever its relation to parallel human endeavors—such as the history of which it is part, such as criticism and historiography—literature remains a figment of man's intellect and psychology, as "real" as he can make it.

Is courtly love then purely literary? If it were so, would it be a mere style sheet for amorous rhetoric, for *sic et non* debates and palinodic dissertations? Or is it a more noble thing, which when placed in tandem with "martial valor" combines harmoniously with it to become the "chivalry topos" in medieval romance?[5] Might it be, as Rupert Pickens wondered at an earlier meeting of our society, just one literary *matière* among many?[6] We need not expect uniformity among literary definitions of courtly love, which, like any doctrine, takes on particular nuances with changing times and places.

Or is courtly love not solely literary, but a phenomenon so real as to express psychological truths that may escape the archives and chronicles, so widespread as to embody "un secteur du coeur, un des aspects éternels de l'homme,"[7] from Egypt of the second millennium B.C. onward? Does it follow that it is a permanent, popular vein of human feeling that surfaces—now here, now there—in written texts, much as oral folk motifs are incorporated into countless medieval works? Or is it all of these and more, if, as has been said, "there is not one courtly love but twenty or thirty of them"?[8]

If we accept for the moment that there are in fact many courtly loves, at least some of them will have a supra-literary reality. Even the tempting "game theory" of courtly literature admits that the game of love is played with some seriousness in the societies that sponsor and witness it. As an intellectual system with a formalized code, and as "a mode of thought, expressed in literary conventions" and revealing "a cluster of personal feelings and social values,"[9] it most surely had a psychological reality. Roger Boase views the impact of courtly love in the very broadest terms: "Courtly love was . . . a comprehensive cultural phenomenon, a literary movement, an ideology, an ethical system, a style of life, and an expression of the play element in culture which arose in an aristocratic Christian environment exposed to Hispano-Arabic influences."[10] The essays in this volume largely reflect all the aspects of this panoramic view.

Most, if not all, of the twelve contributors to this volume speak specifically of courtly love; and each knows what he and others mean by it. All would appear willing to concur with Eugène Vinaver's approach to the term—that it "does represent something for which no more convenient name has been found" and which, at least in the twelfth century, "is not a coherent, systematic doctrine, not a fixed set of rules of behavior, but rather the means of discovering fascinating and insoluble problems concerning the psychology and ethics of love."

Scholarly discussions, from romantic to structuralist, often reveal more about the century of the scholar than about the subject of his investigation. Today we are participants in the latest stage in the history of medievalism; that future opinion might identify more closely with Gaston Paris than with viewpoints we hold dear is cause for humility and patience. For the present at least, we wish to suggest a moratorium on the circular, often self-sustaining, and ever more finely pared and specialized speculations on the sources of courtly love and its reality or nonreality, in hopes that the Fifth or Sixth Triennial Congress of the ICLS may be ready to open once again the dossier at a time when the "fragmentation due to specialization"[11] in current courtly love scholarship may have abated.

It is time we look with new eyes upon the weave, the texture, and the design of courtly literature. At another recent ICLS gathering, Harry F. Williams proposed that courtly literature be considered as that literature espousing courtly love, this latter being "any kind of elevated human love which holds center stage."[12] Courtly literature would then encompass, in the examples Williams provides, "the love songs of the troubadours and trouvères, any of the romances of Chrétien de Troyes except the *Perceval*, only the first part of the *Roman de la Rose*"—and of course the many similar and related works in Provençal, French, and the other medieval vernaculars.

The varied topics within the present volume suggest the possibility of extending Williams's definition. The earlier literature that forthrightly portrays courtly love is a foundation which, whether treated reverently or lightly, as matter or as form, becomes the common referent for the European literary works discussed in this volume. Indeed, the papers chosen stress these continuing responses, the evolutions and translocations that tell us as much about the nature of the early works of "pure" courtly literature as the latter's own most perfect paradigms do. Spiritualizations, satires, and even outright rejections of courtly literature may all be considered together as parts of one complex tradition. We are then of one mind with Peter Dronke, who believes "that researches into European courtly poetry should . . . be concerned with the variety of sophisticated and learned *development* of *courtois* themes, not with seeking specific origins for the themes themselves." [13]

Dronke's well-turned phrase, intended to spur on studies in this new direction, corresponds to our own concern with "expansion and transformations." The two phenomena are, in our view, simultaneous and inseparable. The general movement from the troubadours to the trouvères, to the minnesingers, to the *dolcestilnovisti*, represents a geographical expansion with its inevitable transformations in attitudes; the profound transformations in attitudes from the time of Chrétien to that of Chaucer, Dunbar, or Spenser reflect the equally inevitable influences of different cultures and societies.

One recurring problem of categorizing or pigeonholing courtly literature comes from the fact that its most usual basic ingredient, courtly love, started out being the ideal of "a refined, perhaps impossible, transformation of a stubborn, basic passion." [14] This remarkable transformation was soon in turn transformed. From the idealized and idolized but still secular *domna*, the step to a properly religious image was a small one. The elements of the love service and its accompanying conventions, interpreted neutrally or *in malo* by some, were as easily utilized *in bono* by others. Dante's Beatrice is well on the way to apotheosis, while the *domna* has already become the Virgin for several of Dante's Iberian predecessors and near-contemporaries: Gonzalo de Berceo (in Castilian), Alfonso X, *el Sabio* (in Galician-Portuguese), and Ramon Llull (in Catalan).

Yet the *bonum* and *malum* are not always clearly distinguishable. In the *Libro de buen amor*, the fourteenth-century masterpiece by Spain's Juan Ruiz, *buen amor* and its opposite *loco amor* are expressed and portrayed as inextricably bound up together, providing endless ambiguities which the author invites the intelligent reader to sort out for himself. We would do well, beset with such manifold transformations of courtly love and literature, to follow Vinaver's suggestion and see not a fatal tension but a fruitful ambiguity in medieval courtly literature. Common forms, imagery, and rhetoric are, in successive hands, turned to often conflicting and contradictory ends along a scale ranging from seduction and sin at one extreme to serenity and salvation at the other. Any literature or literary work giving center stage to the courtly content and style—for whatever purpose, even an anticourtly one—is then courtly.

A further condition should be added; namely, the support and appreciation of the refined audience generally associated with aristocratic courts. Lacking such an audience, courtly convention and tradition rapidly atrophy and wither away. As a working definition for courtly literature, we would propose that it is a body of literature, dependent upon the audiences of the secular intelligentsia, which exemplifies, imitates, expands, or transforms those literary traditions focusing on elevated forms of love and related psychological phenomena and drawing on specific constellations of form and style rooted in twelfth-century Provençal and French works.

There is a particular transformation we have not yet considered: that of genre. There is substantial reason to believe that courtly expression begins as lyric-based, but it soon pervades other forms. The general progress from the individual *canso* toward cyclical arrangements like the *Cantigas de Santa Maria*, the *Vita nuova*, and the Petrarchan *Canzoniere* finds its prose parallel in the development, through courtly romance, of early forms of the novel. One such vital moment, analyzed by Lowanne Jones in this volume, occurs in the thirteenth century when the biographical or allegorical narrative enlarges the horizons and the potential audience of the lyric while clearing the way to the Renaissance novella. The movement toward "cohesion" in later medieval fiction, discerned by Eugène Vinaver, is one point on this trajectory. Seen from the standpoint of genre, seven of the articles in this collection may be classified as dealing primarily with narrative, while three are concerned more with lyrical or satirical poetry, one with the early secular theater, and the remainder with problems of cultural transmission, courtly love, and the study of the courts themselves. Whether the transferal of an originally lyric situation into other genres imposes a resolution of tension and hence devitalizes the courtly paradox,[15] or whether on the contrary ambiguity continues to mark the greatest representatives of the courtly ethos will be one underlying theme of the following contributions. A word now about the order in which the articles are presented. The first three, posing the crucial problem of ambiguity, collectively suggest that the modern critic must exercise caution in analyzing medieval literary situations according to modern doctrines or to modern ideas of medieval dogma. The varied approaches to a common thematic configuration, as for example in the multiple versions of the Lancelot and Tristan stories, here studied by Vinaver and Wiesmann-Wiedemann, demonstrate the ambiguous role that even characteristic features—for example, the adulterous element—play in the evolution of the story as it reinvents itself in new times and new places. Furthermore, these two studies remind us, at a time when such caveats are welcome, that we must not misrepresent the complex medieval world view through too narrow a perspective or too simplistic a credo. As Chrétien de Troyes's works sowed seeds of discord among modern scholars, so the symbolic dilemma and conflicting loyalties of Lancelot, Guenevere, and Arthur, or Tristan, Isolde, and Mark, led to many of the purposely equivocal situations studied later in the volume. "Did only one spirit of the Middle Ages exist, one party line?" Emphatically not, for, as William Calin remarks, "the Middle Ages were an extraordinarily rich and complex period."

The next two articles offer individual but complementary studies of important cultural landmarks of twelfth-century France—courtly literature's formative period and area. Terence Scully's revelation that the *joie de la cort* in *Erec* represents none other than *fin' amor* and Matilda Tomaryn

Bruckner's demonstration of how specific episodes were interwoven under the guiding principles of repetition and variation show with what rapidity and skill the courtly ethos and techniques were established, refined, extended, and renewed.

The following six articles describe the expansion and transformations of courtly literature in other centuries and societies: in thirteenth-century Occitan literature (Lowanne Jones), in Dante and Petrarch (Sara Sturm-Maddox), in the late fourteenth-century *Griseldis* play (Donald Maddox), in Chaucer (John Bowers), in the Scottish poet William Dunbar (Florence Ridley), and in Edmund Spenser (Winifred Keaney).

This variety pays tribute to the ingenuity of our European courtly writers. From Dante's inflection of the *joy d'amor* toward the *directio voluntatis*, from his mingling of courtly and mystical loves up to Dunbar's satires on the debasement of courtliness, a whole world passes before our eyes. One important theme among many is that of the relation between love and arms, brought out notably by Maddox and throughout Bowers's and Keaney's contributions. Does love encourage or inhibit valor? The question and a whole gamut of solutions date back to the beginning: to the *romans d'antiquité* and to Chrétien de Troyes.

Finally, the keystone of the edifice is William Melczer's banquet address. It retains enough of its original oral delivery style to evoke, for all who were then present, memories of its plain good sense. Here we return to some of the problems, explicit and implicit, raised by the earlier articles and to the always provocative relations between literature and history. For if we neglect Melczer's counsel that "literature is the indirect, often imperfect, and always kaleidoscopic reflection of an underlying *reality*," our literary debates deserve to be denounced and boycotted by our colleagues in the historical disciplines. Melczer's address could well have opened this volume, but we thought it best that its stirring call for greater interdisciplinary efforts by teams of scholars should sound a final, hopeful note as this foray into the development of the courtly mode comes to its close. It is a call entirely in tune with the mood of the individual scholars who gathered in Athens, Georgia; it represents well the design and scope of the ICLS Congress and echoes the goals of the society. We sincerely hope that such a noble proposal for interdisciplinary, international teamwork will not go long unanswered.

NOTES

1. Notably Joan M. Ferrante and George D. Economou, eds., *In Pursuit of Perfection: Courtly Love in Medieval Literature* (Port Washington, N.Y.: Kennikat, 1975); R. G. Collins and John Wortley, eds., *On the Rise of the Vernacular Literatures in the Middle Ages, Mosaic*, vol. 8, no. 4 (1975); Peter Haidu, ed., *Approaches to Medieval Romance*, Yale French Studies, no. 51 (New Haven, 1975).

2. Francis X. Newman, ed., *The Meaning of Courtly Love* (Albany: State University of New York Press, 1968). Major review articles include Charles Camproux, in "Chronique," *Revue des Langues Romanes* 79 (1970): 469–78; Jean Frappier, "Sur un procès fait à l'amour courtois," *Romania* 93 (1972): 145–93; Francis L. Utley, "Must We Abandon the Concept of Courtly Love?" *Medievalia et Humanistica*, n.s. 3 (1972): 299–324; Karl D. Uitti, "Remarks on Old French Narrative: Courtly Love and Poetic Form (I)," *Romance Philology* 26 (1972–73): 77–93.

3. *Fin' amor* is the troubadours' usual term; *amour troubadouresque* is proposed by Camproux (p. 478), who sees the *amour courtois* exemplified in *Lancelot* as having no useful application in the troubadours; *amour chevaleresque* was used by Fauriel (see Uitti, p. 78); *noble love* is extrapolated from D. D. R. Owen's title *Noble Lovers* (New York: New York University Press, 1975), *medieval love* is favored, as an all-encompassing term, by Utley (p. 317).

4. Ferrante and Economou, p. 3.

5. Robert W. Hanning, "The Social Significance of Twelfth-Century Chivalric Romance," *Medievalia et Humanistica*, n.s. 3 (1972): 3–29, cited pp. 3–4.

6. Rupert T. Pickens, "The Game of Love as *Matière*," annual meeting of the American-Canadian Branch of ICLS, MLA convention, New York, 28 December 1973, pp. 7–8 (scheduled for publication in a volume entitled *Medieval Eros*, edited by P. Aloysius Thomas).

7. Henri-Irénée Marrou, "Au dossier de l'amour courtois," *Revue du Moyen Age Latin* 3 (1947): 81–89, cited p. 89; endorsed by Peter Dronke, *Medieval Latin and the Rise of European Love-Lyric*, 2d ed., 2 vols. (Oxford: Clarendon, 1968), 1: xvii.

8. Utley, p. 323.

9. Ferrante and Economou, p. 3.

10. Roger Boase, *The Origin and Meaning of Courtly Love: A Critical Study of European Scholarship* (Manchester: Manchester University Press; Totowa, N.J.: Rowman and Littlefield, 1977), pp. 129–30.

11. Boase, p. 122.

12. Harry F. Williams, "Towards a Definition of Courtly Literature," ICLS meeting, South Atlantic Modern Language Association, Washington, D.C., 4 November 1977.

13. Dronke, 1: xvii.

14. Robert W. Hanning, review of Ferrante and Economou, *Speculum* 53 (1977): 975–77, cited p. 976.

15. As is held by Ferrante and Economou, pp. 5–9.

Courtly Literature
and the
International Legends

Landmarks in Arthurian Romance

EUGÈNE VINAVER

If I were to choose a motto for this paper I would suggest the famous lines from the last act of Richard II:

> No thought is contented.
> The better sort, as thoughts of things divine,
> Are intermix'd with scruples and do set
> The word itself against the word (v.v.11–14)

These lines were written four and a half centuries after the first appearance of courtly romance on the European literary scene, and yet they seem to sum up the very essence of the genre that in the hands of poets like Chrétien de Troyes revolutionized the literary life of medieval France and subsequently of the whole of Western Europe.

Thoughts intermixed with scruples were not in themselves a novelty; they had played a prominent part in the composition of some of the great epic poems that antedated the birth of courtly romance by half a century or more. There is perhaps no better example of ambiguity in early narrative poetry than the unresolved conflict between Roland and Oliver, for the poet never tells us which of them was right: "Rolant est proz e Oliver est sage,"*[1] he writes, and because by the standards of feudal chivalry, prowess and wisdom are virtues of equal value. He says in

*Roland is bold, Olivier is wise

the very next line that both Roland and Oliver are men of outstanding valor: "Ambedui unt merveillus vasselage." †

To juxtapose two contrasting ideas or images was by no means an uncommon procedure at a time when no one preached the classical doctrine of unity. What romance added to this practice was the insistence on the elucidation of the theme, the urge to make the problems of human behavior more manifest and the conflicts more articulate, more meaningful. Along with Abelard's device of *sic et non*, romance writers transferred into the secular sphere the scholastic *manifestatio* which helped to make the problems less soluble and the controversies more acute.

The term *courtly love* is, of course, not authentically medieval. We all know that it owes its existence to the nineteenth-century scholar Gaston Paris and that it has been under attack in recent years. But it does represent something for which no more convenient name has been found. What it stands for, so far as twelfth-century poets are concerned, particularly poets like Chrétien de Troyes and his contemporaries, is not a coherent systematic doctrine, not a fixed set of rules of behavior, but rather the means of discovering fascinating and insoluble problems concerning the psychology and ethics of love, problems that are all the more fascinating because they are insoluble. Courtly love in the twelfth century is primarily a matter of controversy, a rich source of dilemma which it is the poet's task to explore, to elucidate and to discuss often from two opposite points of view without necessarily committing himself to either. One major issue which is central to all courtly literature is that of love versus honor. It dominates

† And both of them are marvelously brave

Chrétien's most famous romance *The Story of the Cart* or *The Romance of Lancelot*; and because modern critics, unlike medieval poets, are more interested in seeking solutions than in understanding problems, hardly a year goes by without some solution being found, some new meaning being forced upon that particular work.

The story is that of a rescue which is essentially a chivalric quest and which has two distinct aims: that of delivering Guinevere from her captor Meleagant and that of giving Lancelot the opportunity of exhibiting his valor and his devotion to his lady, the opportunity of proving that he is worthy of her love. The most striking example of Lancelot's commitment to this second purpose of the quest—which might be described as its spiritual purpose—occurs very early in the story, in the scene in which for the first time we see the mysterious figure of a knight walking, followed by his wounded horse, in what he thinks is the direction taken by the abductor of the queen. It is then that he meets a dwarf driving a cart. The cart was in those days the equivalent of the pillory; it was an ignominious vehicle used for carrying prisoners to the place of punishment. Lancelot asks the dwarf if he has seen the queen, and the dwarf offers to take him to the place where he would have early news of her.

Only a momentary hesitation precedes Lancelot's acceptance of this offer, but this momentary hesitation is perhaps the essence of the whole work. What Lancelot has to decide is whether, in order to accelerate the rescue of the Queen, he can legitimately degrade himself by riding in the cart, whether he can sacrifice his honor as a knight for the sake of his duty as a lover. The hesitation here takes the form of a dialogue in Lancelot's mind between two allegorical figures, Reason and Love. It is Reason that counsels Lancelot to refrain from degrading himself, but Reason, the poet tells us, dwells only on the knight's lips, not in his heart: in his heart dwells Love. The dialogue between Reason and Love is symmetrically arranged with six lines devoted to each, and each group of six lines corresponds to one of Lancelot's steps. This crucial dialogue can be described as the scene of Lancelot's two steps, perhaps the most important two steps in the history of literature.

We are not told whether the choice he makes is the right one, but the sequel is not devoid of a certain element of dramatic surprise. When Lancelot, after innumerable trials and adventures and after having defeated Guinevere's captor Meleagant in a fierce battle, is at last admitted to her presence, she receives him coldly and refuses to speak to him. And so he goes away in despair, convinced that it was his acceptance of the dwarf's offer that caused his lady's displeasure and that she is unable to forgive him the loss of chivalric honor which he accepted so readily. He will soon learn that the reason for Guinevere's anger is the reverse: she found fault with his conduct not because he rode in the cart but because he hesitated for two steps before getting into it. The dictates of love, according to her, should not be a matter of debate for a knight-lover: there should not be even a moment's hesitation between the contrasting ideals that were responsible for Lancelot's two steps, Love and Reason. Reason must yield to Love without question, without creating in the lover's mind anything that could be described as a moral dilemma. Not many people in the story, apart from Guinevere herself and ultimately Lancelot, hold this view. Most of those who see Lancelot in the cart think he has disgraced himself and some of them despise him for it. And so we are left to wonder what it is that Lancelot ought to have done. Was it right or was it wrong for him to hesitate? We don't really know.

And here I must pause to consider the aesthetic implications of this state of affairs. We see nothing abnormal or even unusual in modes of thinking which allow contradictions to remain unresolved—we are quite prepared to listen to an argument developed on the lines of *Sic et non*. But when it comes to a serious work of fiction we regard any unanswered question as an artistic imperfection. Why? Simply because we have been brought up to believe that each work must have one central meaning. And so we cannot rest until we have decided which side Chrétien was on: on the side of chivalry or on the side of courtly love conceived as total dedication to the service of the beloved no matter what sacrifices such a service may involve. And because Chrétien's supreme artistry enables us to make a perfect case for either interpretation, critics since the turn of the century have been having a glorious time pulling now in one direction, now in the other—fighting as they so often do over a nonexistent issue. If only they had paid attention to the fact that ambivalence figures prominently in medieval lyric poetry and fiction as a source of inspiration and of pleasurable emotion, they would have realized the irrelevance of their approach and we would all have been spared many tiresome controversies. Like all writers of courtly romance, Chrétien aims at an explicit presentation of the central problem of his work—so explicit, in fact, that it appears insoluble. Lancelot may have hesitated for only two steps before getting into the cart, but in the reader's mind the hesitation is meant to go on indefinitely, and the romance itself will not answer the question of what the right thing was for Lancelot to do.

There is one type of work in which a modern reader admits this kind of situation and that is tragedy, in which the tragic dilemma itself can become a unifying factor and can act as an emotional and conceptual center. Nothing of the kind happens in Chrétien's *Lancelot*; there is nothing there that could be called tragic. Lancelot may experience great distress after having been rebuked by Guinevere, but he is soon comforted when he discovers the real reason for her coldness and when at last he realizes how he was at fault from her point of view. What we have to accept is an aesthetic situation in which an insoluble problem instead of being a source of tragedy becomes one of intellectual enjoyment. And once we have accepted this we shall understand why, while going through many trials and tribulations, Arthurian characters in the early romances never cast a dark shadow on the smiling landscape in which they move.

Half a century elapsed before Lancelot appeared again in a work of fiction, this time in the spacious *Roman de Lancelot du Lac*, a prose romance that formed the central and by far the most ambitious part of the great Arthurian prose cycle produced between the years 1220 and 1225. The landscape continues to be bright and smiling but no longer for the same reasons: Lancelot and Guinevere seem to have left their courtly dialectics far behind. They now live in a world in which it seldom occurs to anyone to contrast reason and love.

A perfectly consistent philosophy of love and honor takes the place of unresolved controversies—a process that bears some resemblance to contemporary developments in the field of theological thinking. A story such as the episode of the cart could find little justification in a work that makes every effort to show within the considerably widened boundaries of Arthur's realm how love and honor can serve to exalt one another. At the same time, however, the episode was too much a part of the known story of Lancelot to be left out. So the prose writer reproduced it accurately but gave it a new motivation. Lancelot hesitates to get into the cart because he does not know whether he can trust the dwarf. In this way the initial dilemma is avoided. The degrading nature of the vehicle is deliberately played down, Lancelot is not concerned about his loss of honor, and the entire episode is transferred from the original spiritual level of the quest to its adventurous or narrative level.

But what of Guinevere's displeasure, which is also part of the episodic content of the romance? It too is there, but again the motivation is altered. She is angry with Lancelot for two hitherto unknown reasons: he left the court without asking her permission; and, as a result of Morgan le Fay's extraordinary machinations involving the use of the supernatural, he has parted with Guinevere's ring. The queen thinks that she has reason to be jealous, but the misunderstanding is soon cleared up and all ends well.

Not that the cultivation of controversy as an intellectual pastime and an artistic device had suddenly ceased. On the contrary, it continued, sometimes even in more acute form than ever before, but the problems that attracted the

attention of thirteenth-century writers were not the same
as earlier. They were if anything of wider significance, and
the practice of leaving them unresolved had considerably
more serious consequences for all concerned. The antinomy of love and honor which had proved to be an inex-
haustible source of lively argument in courtly lyric and
early romance gives way to a harmonious view of chivalric
life—a change that fully accounts for the new version of
the cart episode. But as one antinomy goes, another takes
its place, another category of "thoughts intermix'd with
scruples." There is in the French Arthurian cycle a fundamental dichotomy fully developed in the last branches: the
divine chivalry of the Grail on the one hand and the earthly
chivalry of the Round Table, Corbenic, and Camelot on
the other. So far any attempt made to reduce the Grail
theme and the Arthurian theme proper to a harmonious
synthesis has proved futile.

What is characteristic of the work as a whole is the deliberate sharpening of the contrast, setting the two worlds
—that of the Grail and that of Arthur—against one another. Divine grace symbolized by the Grail is accorded to
the pure knight Galahad and to a lesser extent to his two
close companions, Perceval and Bors, but is withheld from
the greatest of all Arthurian heroes, Lancelot. No one can
tell which of the two ideals should dominate the other,
with the result that it was possible for Paolo and Francesca
to be the victims of the enchanting prose of the Lancelot
romance in the famous scene describing the first kiss of
Lancelot and Guinevere and "to read that day no more"
(*Inf.*, v.138), just as it is possible for some modern readers

to interpret the entire cycle in terms of the Grail theme alone. No one can claim to have understood its meaning who fails to see simultaneously the two facets of the work and to derive from their juxtaposition the kind of enjoyment that a true artistic experience can provide. And if the work has remained virtually unknown in modern times it is not simply because of its length and complexity but because it presupposes in the reader the ability to savor a contrast without seeking to reconcile the two sides, the readiness to contemplate two boldly juxtaposed ideals.

Nor is there any tragic sense about their juxtaposition, any more than there is in the earlier forms of romance. The author uses multiple motivation, so that each important event is accounted for in a variety of ways—an arrangement which rules out the tragic concept of a single determining cause.

The remarkable thing is, however, that the ideological cleavage does not interfere in any way with the careful planning and scrupulously coherent structure of the narrative. It is in fact one of the most fully integrated compositions of its kind. It is an elaborate and a wonderfully well thought-out *Summa* of various, often heterogeneous themes which the twelfth century had bequeathed to the writers of the new age, a work inspired by a consistent desire to establish connections where none had existed before and to show how any given tradition could acquire added interest by being linked with others. It was in this work that the Grail became part of the Lancelot romance, for the Grail hero here is not Perceval, but Galahad, Lancelot's son. This is only one of a great number of material links between the courtly world of Lancelot and the spiritual world of the Grail. The movement toward greater cohesion, so typical of late medieval fiction, was nowhere more manifest than in the narrative technique of the Arthurian prose cycle.

And yet this urge to establish coherent relationships at the narrative level coexists with an equally strong tendency to accentuate contrasts on the ideological level—a significant discrepancy between the treatment of the *matter* and the *meaning*, the coherence of the former and the deliberate ambiguity of the latter—an ambiguity that most of us still find difficult to accept. When Ferdinand Lot published his book on the prose *Lancelot* and established the pattern of its narrative texture,[2] many of us felt that this was a challenge to find a corresponding degree of coordination at the ideological level—to discover the common spiritual denominator for the major themes of the work. Myrrha Lot-Borodine and many others after her displayed great ingenuity in trying to reconcile the two, but all to no purpose. Galahad and Lancelot to this day resist any attempt to treat them as facets of a single spiritual entity. No such entity exists except in the minds of people who are incapable of seeing the validity of two contrasting philosophies, a regrettable and typically modern limitation imposed upon us by our outmoded literary conventions.

It was in this complex and highly sophisticated form that Arthurian romance reached Sir Thomas Malory, the last and the greatest of medieval Arthurian writers, while he was composing his *Book of Sir Lancelot and Queen Guinevere*, which was to be followed by the greatest of all his

books, *The Tale of the Death of King Arthur*. On a superficial level he merely dramatized the traditional stories and
gave them a more realistic coloring. Lancelot meets a cart
driven by two woodcutters who have been sent by Meleagant to the forest to fetch wood. It is clearly not the cart
used to carry prisoners to the place of punishment. Neither
Guinevere nor Lancelot is concerned about its possible significance. Far from hesitating to get into it Lancelot orders
the two men to let him ride in it, and upon their refusal he
strikes one of them with his mailed gauntlet and kills him.
The other woodcutter, seeing what has happened and fear-
ing for his own life, offers to take Lancelot wherever he
wants to go. And as Lancelot triumphantly jumps into the
cart the long history of this episode is concluded in a way
which would have surprised its original inventor.

It is a far cry from the allegorical debate between Reason
and Love to the brutal killing of the woodcutter, but we
must remove once and for all from our minds any notion
of Malory's direct connection with the original form of
Arthurian romance and particularly with Chrétien de
Troyes. Like his contemporaries Malory was a reader of
prose romances not of the Arthurian verse romances of the
twelfth century. The transition from the latter to the former had been a spectacular change from fantasy to tangible
reality. So that when Malory came to his high theme,
what he had before him was not an allegorical vision of
chivalric rescue but a whole world of complex human relationships, of conflicts and conquests, passions and friend-
ships, great deeds and heroic sacrifices. And as I have just
said, in that vast composition embodying the whole his-

tory of Arthurian fellowship from its foundation to its downfall as well as a variety of other themes and motifs old and new, the remarkably skillful coordination of disparate episodes and characters at the narrative level went hand in hand with the unresolved antinomy of earthly and divine chivalry. This is precisely what is so alien to the modern mind and indeed to Malory's temperament as a storyteller.

Malory's work, in spite of its outward resemblance to the earlier forms of Arthurian fiction, is in fact a complete negation of the two principles upon which the French prose romances were based. At the narrative level he makes little attempt to imitate, let alone reproduce, the system of cross links, references, echoes, and anticipations which forms the sophisticated fabric of his French models, while at the ideological level he fails to see how one can glorify both Lancelot and Galahad and at the same time recognize the spiritual cleavage between them. He can see no essential difference between the chivalry of Lancelot and that of his son Galahad. He even thinks that the sword that Merlin left for Lancelot, the sword of fratricide, could be used equally well by Galahad. The result is a work from which one can deduce a simple and coherent philosophy of chivalric behavior but no consistent design linking the various episodes with one another, a work consisting of many noble tasks, unified much more by their spirit than by their matter.

Thus the two most characteristic features of medieval romantic fiction vanish from the Arthurian scene; but in their place something new and vital arises which confers true greatness upon Malory's work: an awareness of the tragic potential inherent in human passions and loyalties. The discovery and the fulfillment of this potential occurs in Malory's last book, *The Most Piteous Tale of the Morte Arthur sauns guerdon*, and the transformation of romance into a tragic prose tale is achieved by the seemingly simple process of isolating one vital theme from a number of concomitant themes. What Malory does is to place in the center of things the one single cause of what Caxton calls so startlingly the "dolorous deth and departyng out of thys world of them al" (III.1260n.),[3] namely Lancelot's inability to choose between the two loyalties by which he is equally bound; loyalties not to abstract ideals of honor and love but to real people: Guinevere, Arthur, Gawain and the whole Fellowship of the Round Table. Hence the fatal contrast between Lancelot and Gawain, the irony of Gawain's death caused by a wound received from Lancelot, and finally the downfall of Arthur's kingdom. As in ancient Greek theater, tragedy is born here out of the concentration of the resources of language and thought upon an individual fate torn out of its original epic or cosmic content, a destiny that in virtue of its isolation can no longer be dissolved in an all embracing harmony of a vast mythical universe.

This was not William Caxton's idea of the book that he published in 1485—"thys noble and Ioyous book entytled le morte Darthur." He hoped that his readers would find in it enough variety of incident and character to see the story of the death of Arthur in a wide perspective in which joy and sadness would be balanced against each other. In so doing he distorted Malory's tragic vision and impressed upon the English-speaking world an image of Arthurian chivalry in which the "dolorous death and departing" is merely one incident among many. It is perhaps time that we began to see the work of a great prose writer in its true light and the history of Arthurian romance as an example of how the alchemy of art can change the pageantry of chivalric life with its decor of ever green woods and mead-- ows into the human reality of Malory's most piteous *Tale* by the magic of simplification of structure and language.

Malory is probably the first writer to have brought the language of romance so close to ordinary speech and one of the few to realize that in order to speak to us convincingly, tragedy needs only the simple words of everyday life. Witness, for example, the relentless power of un-adorned statement such as the brief remark that concludes the description of Lancelot's grief over the deaths of Arthur and Guinevere: "and there was no comfort that the Bysshop, nor syr Bors, nor none of his felowes coude make hym, it avaylled not" (III.1257).

Such is the last and perhaps the finest landmark in the long history of Arthurian romance, obscured by later adapters and even more by commentators, few of whom have noticed the changing panorama of the medieval liter-ary scene. The great event brought about by the artistry of the last medieval Arthurian writers was the emergence of a new artistic vision from the old. To understand the full significance of this event and to experience it we have to see the work both in its aesthetic immediacy and as part of a complex historical process: two approaches which correspond to the two dimensions of any artistic achieve-ment—two powerful sources of light thanks to which the

Tale of the Death of King Arthur appears in sharp relief as the conclusion of one great tradition and the first step toward another.

NOTES

1. Joseph Bédier, ed., *La Chanson de Roland* (Paris: H. Piazza, 1937). The translation has been taken from *Song of Roland*, trans. Robert Harrison (New York: New American Library, 1970), p. 85, l. 1093.

2. Ferdinand Lot, *Etude sur le Lancelot en prose* (Paris: E. Champion, 1918).

3. Eugène Vinaver, ed., *The Works of Sir Thomas Malory*, 2d ed., 3 vols. (Oxford: at the University Press, 1967).

Defense and Illustration of *Fin' Amor*

Some Polemical Comments
on the Robertsonian Approach

WILLIAM CALIN

As a professor of French literature, I do my work without mishap. Although as a general rule my colleagues in the modern centuries know little about the Medium Aevum, they pay it great honor, for it is alleged to be difficult. They even presume my field to be exotic and devious, especially if their enrollments fall beneath mine. But when I chat with colleagues in the English department, it is a different story. Guillaume de Lorris is likely to be more meaningful to them than is Racine, and William the Conqueror at Hastings makes up part of their culture, even if they have never heard of Henry IV or Léon Blum. Imagine my consternation these last few years when they inform me that, like Santa Claus, there is no courtly love, or that the very nature of medieval studies has been revolutionized once and for all by a man who teaches Chaucer at Princeton. Although I sometimes find it difficult to cope with statements that put my weltanschauung in jeopardy, on the other hand, such "heresies" can be salutary to the life of our church: hence this essay.

The approach to medieval texts called indifferently "allegorical," "typological," "exegetic," or "Robertsonian," in honor of its most eminent exponent, is no doubt the major innovation in medieval *Anglistik* circles over the last twenty years. This methodology states that the insights one normally brings to the study of sacred texts, especially Holy Writ, may also be employed fruitfully for the analysis of medieval secular literature. The assumption of a common medieval *mentalité*, religiously oriented, leads to an outrightly "clerical" reading not only of the *Chanson de Roland*, Dante's *Commedia*, and *Piers Plowman*, but also of works as disparate, as seemingly profane, as Andreas Capellanus's *De Amore*, romances by Chrétien de Troyes, love-allegories of Guillaume de Lorris and Jean de Meun, and the entire opus of Chaucer: *The Miller's Tale*, *The Reeve's Tale*, and *The Merchant's Tale* in addition to *The Knight's Tale* and *Troilus and Creseyde*. As for *fin' amor*, we are told that it is a "modern" concept that can only be an "impediment to the understanding of medieval texts," for no medieval Christian author could possibly have encouraged his public to indulge in idolatrous passion, in irrational concupiscence.[1]

I should like to take up two minor points before proceeding to discuss the fundamental reasons why I consider the extreme Robertsonian approach untenable.

Point 1: the claim that courtly love is a modern invention, specifically the creation of Gaston Paris, professor at the Collège de France, who was the first human being to employ the term *amour courtois*, in an article on Chrétien's *Lancelot* published in 1881.[2] Admittedly, the medievals did not speak of *amour courtois*. But they did speak of *fin' amor* or *bon' amor*, to be distinguished from *fol' amor*; and these terms that designate secular, profane, heterosexual love recur frequently in Old and Middle French and Occitan texts. Although Paris did not specifically say so (alas!), his term *amour courtois* was probably as much a modern "translation" from the Old French as an intellectual neologism on his part. In any case, whatever we think of the word, the concept and the literary reality behind it are real enough. Indeed I submit that it is extremely difficult for one who has perused one hundred *romans courtois*, dozens of courtly allegories, and courtly lyrics in the thousands, so many of which speak of *fin' amor* and scrutinize it with no built-in negative value-judgments, to claim that only one pattern of love exists in the Middle Ages: *caritas* and its antitype *cupiditas*. We would do well to ponder the speech of Lady Reason to the Lover in the *Roman de la Rose*, in which she insists that the "thing" exists; whether we call it *coilles* or *reliques* makes no difference at all.[3]

Point 2: the claim that a love ethos based on adultery is inconceivable in our Western, Christian Middle Ages.[4] C. S. Lewis numbered adultery as one of the four distinguishing traits of *fin' amor*. More recent scholars have, in contrast, listed numbers of works or whole literary traditions in which boy marries girl in the end, and these scholars have pointed out that in "real life" medieval man frowned upon adultery, citing the appropriate articles of canon law and charters from the annulment courts. All well and good. But from this to jump to the conclusion that *fin' amor* never existed at all—in fact or in story—is quite another matter. C. S. Lewis was a great critic, a great medievalist, and a distinguished man of letters. He also wrote *The Allegory of Love* in 1936. It is natural that almost a half-century later some of his ideas have to be revised; by revising them we do not necessarily condemn him, his book, or his doctrine in toto. Furthermore, for whatever it is worth, C. S. Lewis is hardly better known on the Continent than D. W. Robertson. Our European colleagues have developed their own theories on *fin' amor*, with or without adultery; whatever their views, many of them do not consider adultery to be the keystone of medieval erotic literature. My own opinion is the following: adultery is present in the two greatest legends of *fin' amor*—the stories of Tristan and Lancelot. Adultery also exists as an assumed backdrop for many lyrics of the Occitan troubadours. On the other hand, a large number of courtly romances, and even courtly allegories, tell of love between youth and maiden which will end in deflowering, even marriage, but where no potential or actual *cornuto* appears on the scene. Essential to *fin' amor* is the notion of obstacle—which may or may not be embodied in a *gilos* or *maritz*—and of highly intense, passionate, personal involvement between two people of opposite sexes. Whether either is married and whether or how often the sex act occurs are not essential matters but only, to employ medieval jargon, mere accidents.

When John V. Fleming, referring to the *Roman de la Rose*, makes a statement such as "I cannot conceive of a convincing interpretation of the most popular poetic work of late medieval Christendom which will not be 'Christian,'"[5] he is guilty of more than one fundamental error both in reasoning and in historical interpretation, guilty of what the New Critics used to call fallacies, but what under the circumstances we can just as well designate as heresies. I accuse Robertson, Huppé, and Fleming of the heresy of philosophical predominance and the heresy of univocal zeitgeist. That is, because Augustine of Hippo propounded certain doctrines in the fifth century, and because philosophers cast in his frame of mind taught at the cathedral schools in the twelfth century and at the University of Paris in the thirteenth century, all "serious" works of literature written in those same twelfth and thirteenth centuries have to be interpreted in Augustinian terms, according to Augustine's own reading of the Bible. And all poems that appear to favor *fin' amor* over *caritas*, or do not mention *caritas* at all (such as Chrétien's *Lancelot* and the *Roman de la Rose*—representative selections from our one hundred *romans courtois* and dozens of courtly allegories) are to be interpreted ironically, for no matter what the plot appears to tell us, no matter what the characters say out loud, the author had to treat them in ironic terms, otherwise he also would be guilty of concupiscent idolatry. More than one scholar of international repute has argued against this heresy, pointing out that the twelfth century already marks a turning away from allegory within theological circles, with a renewed emphasis on the literal level of Scripture; that the new Aristotelian currents prevalent in the thirteenth century diverted thought in different channels; and that typological analysis was reserved not for contemporary writings in the vernacular but exclusively for the study of Scripture and of certain Greco-Roman classics such as the *Aeneid* and the *Metamorphoses*. Dante Alighieri was unique in his claim for a multileveled, allegorical reading of his own *Commedia*; and it is grossly unfair to use him as a touchstone for the entire age.[6] I might also point out that the chief works of literary criticism that date from the age of Chrétien de Troyes and Jean de Meun, the *artes poeticae*, are concerned with figures of speech and rhetorical *topoi*, so that if one must interpret medieval works as the medievals read them, we would do well to look for figures of *amplificatio* instead of Christ figures, for *anaphora* not *caritas*. All this is true. But for me the main issue is the following: did only one spirit of the Middle Ages exist, one party line? And to find it must we turn uniquely to philosophers and theologians, to people like Augustine, Bernard of Clairvaux, Peter Lombard, and Thomas Aquinas?

As I have said elsewhere, the analogous supposition for the modern age would entail that all literature of the neopositivistic secular nineteenth century be interpreted according to the philosophy of Auguste Comte and that all literature of our own existential alienated generation be interpreted according to the doctrines of Jean-Paul Sartre.[7] Alas, given the nature of academe, it is more than probable that five hundred years from now we shall indeed be designated by professors at Princeton or Peking as the Age of Sartre or, perhaps, the Age of Derrida; all our writings will be forced onto the procrustean bed of an imposed ideology, and our descendants will assume that we all lived existential angst or structuralist paradigms as the major feature of our daily lives. I submit the following: that in this, as in so many other respects, what is true for us is also true for our ancestors. Like the modern centuries, the Middle Ages were an extraordinarily rich and complex period of history: a time of cathedrals and of great feudal castles and town halls, of polyphony in the liturgy and in the secular motet, of crusades, of pilgrimages, and of feudal warfare, the rise of towns, and of a new orientation

toward women and love. It is this complexity and richness of the Middle Ages that is so attractive to us, an age
of Bernard de Clairvaux and of Chrétien de Troyes, of
Thomas Aquinas and of Jean de Meun. No doubt that the
Robertsonian approach corresponds to that of certain
monks of long ago, but the religious orders were not the
only voice in the Middle Ages, thank Cupid, nor are their
descendants the only ones today.

The richness and subtlety of works of literature, medieval or modern, cannot be reduced to or pigeonholed under any one literary methodology. A Comtian approach
may be appropriate to the study of Zola or the Goncourt
brothers; it is surely less so when we choose to investigate
Baudelaire. Sartrian existentialism will be very helpful to
the readers of, say, Jean-Paul Sartre, but less to those of us
who wish to understand André Breton or Saint-John
Perse. Personally I esteem the typological method, as one
among many ways of seeing deeply into literature, and I
have used it gratefully and with profit.[8] It is not the method itself but rather the unicity, the intolerance, the totalitar-
ian stance of certain orthodox Robertsonians that is most
exasperating. After all, the usual Freudian, or Jungian, or
phenomenologist, or structuralist, or even Marxist does
not claim that he has exclusive rights to truth and that all
other approaches are inherently in error. Not so for Robertson's pupil who employs the following vocabulary to
designate the scholars, of international standing, with
whom he disagrees: "fundamentally wrongheaded," "ob-
fuscating," "nonsensical," "preposterous," "perverse,"
"debilitating," "ludicrous," "cavalier."[9] I cite only the
adjectives, not the nouns.

One reason, perhaps the dominant one, why certain tenants of the Robertsonian school tend to be so dogmatic derives from the fact that it claims indeed not to be a critical approach like others (Freudian, Jungian, phenomenological, structuralist, etc.), not to be a critical approach at all, but instead to possess a unique insight into history, to be history.

It is no accident that Fleming takes more than one swipe at Wellek and Warren, the emblem for modern criticism in old-fashioned English departments, and that Robertson himself consistently castigates other Chaucerians for imposing a "modern reading" on medieval texts. Curiously enough, the same "revisionism," the same skepticism in the face of modern methods, the same refusal to accept a reading of a medieval text that the medievals themselves would not have endorsed or recognized, is to be found in the European countries, among Old French scholars, but almost exclusively those over fifty years of age and devoted to traditional philology and text-editing. In the summer of 1976 at the Société Rencesvals Congress I made some remarks in defense of modern criticism vis-à-vis the *chanson de geste*: at the risk of repeating myself in our Germanic vernacular, I think they are no less valid in a *fin' amor* context.

The Robertsonian historism is based upon two fundamental presuppositions, both of which are false.

1. *That the Middle Ages and the modern world are totally distinct entities, each with a distinct weltanschauung.* In *A Preface to Chaucer* Robertson seeks "to contrast a dominant medieval convention, the tendency to think in terms of symmetrical patterns, characteristically arranged with reference to an abstract hierarchy, with a dominant modern

convention, the tendency to think in terms of opposites whose dynamic interaction leads to a synthesis." [10] In reply, first of all the school of romanticism—which he cites primarily—is by no means the only nor even the dominant trend in modern literature. Symbolic hierarchical structures appear not only in modern poetry and theatre but also in modern romance and modern picaresque. A case can be made that neorealism in the novel and the illusion of sincerity or authenticity in the lyric, like the box stage, like harmony in music and perspective in painting, are anomalies in the history of world culture, that they began sometime in the Renaissance and died with the generation before our own. [11] This means that a simplistic psychological analysis of literary characters is as invalid for the study of modern literature as for medieval, that our age and our most advanced critical methods are perhaps closer to the spirit of the Middle Ages than at any time in the last three hundred years. It is also true that certain presumed hallmarks of the Middle Ages—alchemy, astrology, allegory, typology—persisted well into the eighteenth century and even into our own (witness the Catholic group of poets in France and some recent, arcane creations of the surrealist school) and, therefore, that a Robertsonian approach is quite useful when applied to Spenser and d'Aubigné, to Donne and La Ceppède, to Claudel and Pierre Emmanuel. But no one would claim that the Counter-Reformation, for instance, is uniquely typological in its world view and that the literature of its age preached only one doctrine: *caritas*. To belabor a point, the Middle Ages, the Catholic Renaissance, and our own existential-structuralist mishmash are epochs of multiform variety. And one constant in these three periods is the ideal of romantic love. Indeed, since Dronke and others have sought to demonstrate the persistence of *fin' amor* as an archetype throughout world literature, in ancient Egypt, in classical Japan, in the world of Islam,[12] etcetera, how curious that only our medieval West should be unique, that only with the people who created the myths of Tristan and Iseult, Lancelot and Guinevere, and the allegorical garden of the rose should romantic love be a fallacy invented by Gaston Paris. *Credo quia absurdum.*

2. *That there is an insurmountable opposition between the findings of modern criticism and those of historical scholarship.* Here I am not arguing the point that when history and criticism enter into conflict we have the right to prefer a modern critical reading, because the work of literature is an ontological whole, free in space and time, no longer subject to the age that gave it birth. Nor am I arguing that if Shakespeare and his public would not have understood "our" pattern of rot imagery in *Hamlet*, and Racine and his public would not have understood "our" pattern of master and slave, of torturer and victim, in *Phèdre*, that this is too bad for them because we—that is, Wilson Knight and Northrop Frye, Thierry Maulnier and Roland Barthes— are better critics than Shakespeare and Racine or their publics, and we have legitimate, correct, true insights into their works that they did not and could not have. No, I am not making that argument, though it is a good one, and I leave it for you to meditate on. That is the argument I would have made ten years ago and in fact did; now I claim that the alleged conflict need not exist. This is because much so-called historical scholarship is based upon a nine-

teenth-century positivism that deforms the real spirit of the Middle Ages in strictly historical terms at least as much as does any modern critic. The best contemporary historians (people like Georges Duby and Jacques Le Goff) are returning to a study of the imaginative literature and art of the Middle Ages in order to discover the symbolic and emotional *mentalités* of the age: in the process their insights correspond amazingly to those of modern critics. A Bachelardian approach, a study of the sexual and symbolic implications of fire or water imagery in a medieval poem —*Raoul de Cambrai*, for example, or Machaut's *La Fonteine amoureuse*—is eminently appropriate, since Bachelard, and Jung before him, took their notion of the four elements, with sexual and symbolic connotations from scientific treatises of the Middle Ages. Similarly, a Freudian meditation on Eros and Thanatos is most congruent in a tradition of lyric poets who knew exactly what they were doing when they proclaimed their desire to die for, with, and in their ladies—I am thinking specifically of Scève, Ronsard, and d'Aubigné. Prudish late nineteenth- and early twentieth-century academics were perhaps unfamiliar with *la petite mort*; but we, thanks to Freud and more recent developments, can understand Renaissance poets on our own terms, which also happen to be theirs. Similarly, the structuralist obsession with language and with such notions as a "grammar of narrative" relates them to the tradition of rhetoric so dominant in our culture until the time of the Third Republic. A modern critical reading of a medieval text, as likely as not, will correspond to medieval reality and conform to one aspect of the medieval mind with as much historical validity as the comparable typological interpretation à la Robertson and Huppé.

I shall not presume to define *fin' amor*, nor do I pretend to bring to light new evidence that could improve on someone else's definition. Indeed, it is not certain that definitions of *fin' amor* are likely to be successful—no more and no less so than comparable definitions of other great literary doctrines: symbolism, for example, or surrealism or existentialism or even structuralism. The specialists in the matter are eminently aware that blanket terms serve largely to mask the doctrines and even literary practice of a variety of disparate writers: Sartre, Camus, Merleau-Ponty, Heidegger, and Jaspers; or Barthes, Lévi-Strauss, Genette, Todorov, Althusser, and Lacan. Perhaps the only trait the various French structuralisms have in common is a continued, willed analogy with the terminology of synchronic linguistics; and the only trait that binds American structuralists is a frenetic effort to leap onto the French bandwagon. To return to *fin' amor*, perhaps we should adopt an empirical, inductive attitude: assume that *fin' amor* covers the erotic precepts and actions depicted in the works of literature that refer explicitly to the term or its equivalents. It will then become apparent that there are many quite disparate modes of *fin' amor*: some ascetic and others sensuous, some adulterous and others oriented toward marriage, some laudatory in attitude and others pejorative, some deathly serious and others humorous or ironical. We must not fail to recognize that medieval literature evolves over a period of some four hundred years, that Charles d'Orléans, for example, coming at the end of a tradition, will inevitably treat erotic matters in a riper, more refined, more problematic manner than early *trouvères* such as Gace Brulé and the Châtelain de Coucy. Furthermore, from the very beginning courtly literature inspires criticism and denial: these anticourtly works—the *Roman de Renard*, the fabliaux, part 2 of the *Roman de la Rose*—provide some of the richest and most sophisticated commentary on *fin' amor* and help to measure its place in medieval life and letters. It may still be possible to find traits common to all or most of the courtly love writers: such as, love is an all-encompassing force in a man's life; it makes him a better person; it thrives upon obstacle, and so forth. However, how can one not be impressed by the rich, ambivalent, highly complex treatment that the greatest writers give to *fin' amor*, whether Bernart de Ventadorn, Chrétien de Troyes, Guillaume de Lorris, Guillaume de Machaut, or Charles d'Orléans? Throughout his career, Machaut oscillates between exalting the tradition (in *Le Dit dou Lyon*) or undermining it (in *Le Voir Dit*). The same, no doubt, is true for Chrétien except that recent exegetes have demonstrated that this oscillation, this *sic et non*, is to be found in each of his romances taken separately: that *Cligès* is an anti-Tristan, a neo-Tristan and a super-Tristan at the same time; that *Yvain* and *Lancelot* scrutinize the functioning of passion in marriage and out of it, as a personal and a social experience, with wit and with the highest seriousness.

A final point. As I stated above, Peter Dronke claims that romantic love was not the invention of the twelfth century. Denis de Rougemont showed us that it didn't end with the fall of Constantinople or Granada.[13] De Rouge-

mont's major contribution to our discipline was not espousing the theory of Catharist origins, largely discredited
today, and we can all regret, but should not allow our professional pedantry to overemphasize, the fact that his
knowledge of the *Roman de Tristan* came largely from
Wagner and Bédier not from Béroul and Thomas. None-
theless it is de Rougemont who quite properly emphasized
the continuity of *fin' amor* in our Western tradition: that it
lives on in Dante and Petrarch, in the poets of the Pléiade
and in Shakespeare, in French classicism (Racine, Mme
de La Fayette), in the eighteenth-century novel (Prévost,
Rousseau), in *Madame Bovary*, *Anna Karenina*, and *A la
recherche du temps perdu*. To this I can add the extraordinary
resurgence of romantic love since the First World War: in
the writings of the Surrealists, of course, where Breton's
amour fou is the appropriate modern analogue to, and
translation of, *fin' amor*, and in the poetry of so many great
Frenchmen, whether associated with surrealism or not:
Jouve, Aragon, Eluard, Char, and others. Perhaps the
greatest single long poem of our day is Aragon's *Le Fou
d'Elsa*, which recaptures the spirit of *fin' amor* projected
onto an Islamic scene, presumed by Aragon (and quite a
few medievalists) to be at the origins of the erotic convention. Denis de Rougemont hoped that the tradition of an
exotic, desperate, and adulterous love was reaching the
end of its long life in the middle of our century and would
give way to a healthier, saner relationship between the
sexes. Given the concept of *togetherness* projected on
American television sets in the 1950s and the so-called sexual revolution of the 1970s, de Rougemont may well have
been correct, although not all of us are ecstatically content

with the results. I gather that Manhattan, New York, and Orange County, California, are already dwelling in the post-Christian era, though such is not yet the case in my remote province. However, if I am mistaken, how ironic it would be, from a Robertsonian perspective, that *fin' amor* and Christianity, the last two vestiges of Western civilization as we know it, should perish together in this, our own age of transitions.

NOTES

1. A complete bibliography of the Robertsonian approach would be immense. The seminal booklength essays are: D. W. Robertson, Jr., and Bernard F. Huppé, *Piers Plowman and Scriptural Tradition* (Princeton: Princeton University Press, 1951); Bernard F. Huppé, *Doctrine and Poetry: Augustine's Influence on Old English Poetry* (Albany: State University of New York Press, 1959); D. W. Robertson, Jr., *A Preface to Chaucer: Studies in Medieval Perspectives* (Princeton: Princeton University Press, 1962); Bernard F. Huppé and D. W. Robertson, Jr., *Fruyt and Chaf: Studies in Chaucer's Allegories* (Princeton: Princeton University Press, 1963); Bernard F. Huppé, *A Reading of the Canterbury Tales* (Albany: State University of New York Press, 1964); John V. Fleming, *The Roman de la Rose: A Study in Allegory and Iconography* (Princeton: Princeton University Press, 1969); also the papers collected in *The Meaning of Courtly Love*, ed. F. X. Newman (Albany: State University of New York Press, 1969). The citation in my text alludes to Robertson's essay "The Concept of Courtly Love as an Impediment to the Understanding of Medieval Texts," in *The Meaning of Courtly Love*, pp. 1–18.

2. Gaston Paris, "Etudes sur les romans de la Table Ronde. Lancelot du Lac," *Romania* 10 (1881): 465–96, 12 (1883): 459–534.

3. Guillaume de Lorris and Jean de Meun, *Le Roman de la Rose*, ed. Félix Lecoy, 3 vols. (Paris: Champion, 1965), vol. 1, ll. 7076–95.

4. In addition to several of the works in n. 1 above, cf. John F. Benton, "Clio and Venus: An Historical View of Medieval Love," in *The Meaning of Courtly Love*, pp. 19–42, and the persuasive and intelligent study by Henry Ansgar Kelly, *Love and Marriage in the Age of Chaucer* (Ithaca, N.Y.: Cornell University Press, 1975).

5. Fleming, *The Roman de la Rose*, p. x.

6. Among others, Morton W. Bloomfield, "Symbolism in Medieval Literature," *Modern Philology* 56 (1958–59): 73–81; Leo Spitzer, "Les études de style et les différents pays," in *Langue et littérature. Actes du VIIIᵉ Congrès de la Fédération Internationale des Langues et Littératures Modernes*, Bibliothèque de la Faculté de Philosophie et Lettres de l'Université de Liège, no. 161 (Paris: Société d'Edition "Les belles lettres," 1961), pp. 23–38, esp. p. 32; Jean Misrahi, "Symbolism and Allegory in Arthurian Romance," *Romance Philology* 17 (1963–64): 555–69; Francis Lee Utley, "Robertsonianism Redivivus," *Romance Philology* 19 (1965–66): 250–60.

7. In a review of Fleming's *The Roman de la Rose*, *Speculum* 47 (1972): 311–13.

8. William Calin, *The Epic Quest: Studies in Four Old French Chansons de Geste* (Baltimore: Johns Hopkins Press, 1966), chap. 2; *A Poet at the Fountain: Essays on the Narrative Verse of Guillaume de Machaut* (Lexington: University Press of Kentucky, 1974), chap. 10; *Crown, Cross and Fleur-de-lis: An Essay on Pierre Le Moyne's Baroque Epic Saint Louis*, Stanford French and Italian Studies, no. 6 (Saratoga, Cal.: Anma Libri, 1977), chap. 8; "Structural and Doctrinal Unity in the *Jeu d'Adam*," *Neophilologus* 46 (1962): 249–54; "Cain and Abel in the *Mystère d'Adam*," *Modern Language Review* 58 (1963): 172–76; "Ronsard's Cosmic Warfare: An Interpretation of His *Hymnes* and *Discours*," *Symposium* 28 (1974): 101–18; "Ronsard and the Myth of Justice: A

Typological Interpretation of *Hymne de la Justice*," in *Degré Second* 1 (1977): 1–14.

9. Fleming, *The Roman de la Rose*, pp. vi, 51, 101, 133, 163, 165.

10. Robertson, *A Preface to Chaucer*, p. 6.

11. Françoise Calin and William Calin, "Medieval Fiction and New Novel: Some Polemical Remarks on the Subject of Narrative," *Yale French Studies*, no. 51 (1975): 235–50.

12. Peter Dronke, *Medieval Latin and the Rise of European Love-Lyric*, 2 vols. (Oxford: Clarendon Press, 1965–66); also *The Medieval Lyric* (London: Hutchinson, 1968).

13. Denis de Rougemont, *L'amour et l'Occident* (Paris: Plon, 1939).

From Victim to Villain: King Mark

FRIEDERIKE WIESMANN-WIEDEMANN

In her study of the Tristan story, Joan Ferrante compares corresponding episodes in different versions of the legend, but she treats characters only insofar as they figure within these episodes.[1] This article follows one character, Mark, in order to show how the ethos of different versions and the effect that each work as a whole has on its readers influenced the portrayal of the cuckolded king. Four texts lend themselves to a comparison because they are meant to tell the whole story, even if we lack the complete versions. These are Eilhart, with his feudal point of view; Thomas, with his interest in unhappy love; Gottfried, with his elevation of love to a religious level; and the French *Prose Tristan*, with its simplistic ideology.[2] I concentrate on three points of special importance for assessing Mark's role: his relationship to the lovers, his relationship to King Arthur (who in all versions sides with worldly love), and his relationship to God. In the conclusion, I show to what extent the change in Mark's character is a function of the development in the narrative genre.

In Eilhart's rendition of the legend, at first a strong friendship binds Mark to Tristan, who serves him so well that the king decides not to marry and to leave his kingdom to his nephew. Tristan destroys this tie when he deceives

Mark. The first deception takes place on the wedding night, when Tristan invents the supposed Irish custom of the dark bridal chamber in order to substitute Brangaene for Isolt. Eilhart underlines Tristan's duplicity by commenting that "Tristrant spoke shrewdly to his dear lord" (vv. 2808–9, p. 80) and that "this was the greatest deceit of which Tristrant was ever guilty" (vv. 2838–39, p. 80), for at the same time he lies with Isolt. Tristan is, however, completely excused, for he is a victim of the potion.

From this point on, Mark is shown in a new light. He loses his love and his generosity. It is true that he does not believe the first reports concerning the unlawful love affair, but when he finds the lovers embracing he exclaims: "That is evil love. How can I keep my honor [wereltlîchen êre] . . . ? Since no one should have either joy or sorrow with another's wife, I wouldn't believe it when they told me so often" (vv. 3261–63, 3266–69, p. 85). He is jealous not of Isolt's love but of his honor, of the order of his court and his country.

At the scene of the tryst under the tree, he vacillates. He believes what he sees because he wants to; therefore he appears as a weak character. He restores all Tristan's former privileges, only to let himself be talked into setting another trap; and when he catches his prey his wrath knows no end. His eyes are opened; those he had protected were faithless rebels, disregarding him and everything he stood for as a king. At this moment he sees vengeance as the only solution. Once again his motive is not jealousy but honor. Tristan is to be broken on the wheel and Isolt is to be burned at the stake. Once Tristan has disappeared, thanks to his lucky jump from the chapel, Mark wants to vent his wrath on his wife (vv. 4246–47, p. 96), and he is only too glad to turn her over to the lepers. Here he shows the same lack of moderation that Tristan and Isolt have shown, but unlike the lovers the king is held fully responsible for his actions. Eilhart, through the voice of the people, blames him: "Many people in the country spoke ill of him" (vv. 4298–99, p. 97).

If Mark reacts as a man at this point, his next action is in the role of king and overlord. Finding Tristan and Isolt sleeping in the forest, he places his sword next to his nephew and his glove on his wife. Eilhart does not explain the action, but the tokens Mark leaves are significant. As Jean Marx points out with reference to Béroul's version, the sword and glove represent Tristan's and Isolt's vassalage.[3] Eilhart's poem does not seem to admit any other interpretation, for when Mark lays the glove on Isolt he does not do so to protect her from the sun as in most other versions. His action means not that he forgives her but that he insists on his own rights.

When Mark agrees to resume his married life with Isolt, he tells his counselors that there had been no physical love between Tristan and Isolt, only an exaggerated sentiment of kindness. He feels so threatened by this supposedly innocent love, however, that he refuses to let Tristan live at the court. Does he really believe what he says? Or is his motive purely diplomatic? Why else would he set the wolf trap in a later episode? A king whose wife has been unfaithful loses his dignity; so he does better to pretend that nothing has happened than to repudiate his wife and become the subject of bawdy stories. Mark's lie is motivated not by a personal reason but by *raison d'état*. More than at any other moment in the story, Mark serves the community by removing the only obstacle to its well-being. In opposition to his earlier exaggerated wrath, moderation now characterizes his action. As Eilhart excuses Tristan's and Isolt's deceptions because of the love drink, so Mark's lie may also be excused, for it results from the same desire to keep appearances and it too is caused, in the last analysis, by the potion.

The king's prime concern from this point forth will be to try to prevent Tristan from seeing Isolt. The first time Tristan comes back to Cornwall, in the company of the Arthurian knights, Mark sets the wolf trap. His personality is clearly opposed to that of Arthur: Mark is a king who makes the rules; Arthur is a pawn of his knights. Gawain prolongs the hunt so that Arthur is forced to ask Mark for hospitality; Kay has the idea that all the knights should cut themselves in order to protect Tristan from detection; all that is left for Arthur to do is to look at his limping knights and to explain pitifully to Mark that "they do this all the time" (v. 5440, p. 109).

Again and again Mark pursues Tristan, who keeps coming back to Cornwall, but never is Mark forced to admit his shame publicly. Joan Ferrante explains the lack of the ordeal scene in Eilhart's text by saying: "The absence of God is an indication of Eilhart's antipathy for the love; he alone, of the poets, has no desire to show God's sympathy to the lovers in any way."[4] On the contrary, God is on Mark's side. Ogrin, the representative of God on earth, sends Tristan and Isolt back to Mark, and the king says that if he let Tristan come back to the court, "God would have to despise me" (v. 4932).[5] It is Mark who represents everything that is good and proper. He does not doubt; he does not need the help of an ordeal; he knows and he directs—until the final blow when Isolt leaves her husband and her country, her treasure and her royal robes, all she ever had, and, most of all, her royal honor (vv. 9327–29, 9339, pp. 153–54). But this is also the time when Mark learns about the potion, when he realizes that he has lost not against base faithless feelings but against fate: "It was very foolish of them not to tell me that they had drunk of the fatal [unsêligen] potion and, against their will, were forced to love each other so. Oh, noble queen and dear nephew, Tristrant! I would give you my whole kingdom, people and land, forever for your own if this could bring you back to life" (vv. 9486–97, p. 155). In this final scene Mark is the generous being we had met at the beginning of the poem; more than that, he is a man who knows life, who fights relentlessly for what is right, but who is also aware of human limitations and the power of fate.

Much more than Tristan and Isolt, it is Mark who embodies the human condition, who blindly combats fate, who believes he can order life only to recognize in the end that his struggle had always been hopeless. He surpasses the human condition, however, by humbly acknowledging his limitations and by honoring those who, on a human level, wronged him. That Tristan and Isolt do not reach these heights, that they gave in to fate even though they knew that their behavior was immoral, that they are therefore guilty in spite of their innocence, is symbolized by the intertwining plants on their graves, for as Eilhart tells us "this was due to the power of the potion" (v. 9521, p. 155). Mark, who undergoes a sentimental and political education, becomes a tragic and heroic figure. He is the true victim of the potion, while Tristan and Isolt are but its instruments. Mark, then, is the true hero of Eilhart's poem.

In no other version of the story is the position of the king so exalted. It would appear that Eilhart wrote his poem for an audience less interested in the power of love than in the preservation of the feudal order. By the same token, Eilhart, it seems, did not feel compelled to justify this ethos. There is no discussion of the characters' motives; they act as they must. Thus the poem affects our intellect less than our emotions.

Thomas composed his story for a different audience, "that it may please lovers, and that, here and there, they may find some things to take to heart. May they derive great comfort from it, in the face of fickleness and injury, in the face of hardship and grief, in the face of all the wiles of Love" (fragment Sneyd[2], vv. 833–39, p. 353). The poet is concerned not so much with the feudal ethos as with the ideology of love. Mark is less a king than a lover and, like all the lovers depicted by Thomas, Mark is unhappy.

We understand the power of this love when we learn that Mark empties the vial containing the fatal potion,[6] and later when the poet tells us how Tristan, the two Isolts, and Mark suffer for love: "I do not know what to say here as to which of the four was in greater torment . . . ; let lovers pass their judgement as to who was best placed in love, or who, lacking it, had most sorrow" (fragment of Turin[1], vv. 144–45, 149–51, p. 317).

That his love for Isolt and not his social position moti-

vates Mark's actions becomes clear in the forest scene,
where he lays his glove on Isolt's cheek in order to protect
her from the sun but does not exchange swords, even
though he recognizes the weapon lying between Tristan
and Isolt as the one he had once given to his nephew.[7] He
depends completely on Isolt and so gives up his liberty. He
is a weak, even a ridiculous character. In the orchard scene
he catches Tristan and Isolt *in flagrante delicto*, but afraid of
assuming his responsibility, it seems, he runs out to find
witnesses, giving Tristan enough time to flee. When Brangaene comes to see him in an attempt to spite Isolt, she
tells him: "You are dishonored when you consent to all
her [Isolt's] wishes and suffer her lover about her. . . . I am
well aware why you are dissembling: because you have
not the courage to let her see what you know" (fragment
Douce, vv. 392–94, 399–402, p. 330).[8] Mark loses his
honor, not the worldly honor Eilhart's king claimed but
the honor of a lover.

The true hero of Thomas's story is Tristan. This explains perhaps why we do not learn how Mark reacts to
the death of Tristan and Isolt. The last scene is the touch-
ing one of the dying Isolt clinging to the body of the only
man she has ever loved. No plants intertwine on their
graves, for their love was not a fate thrust upon them but
a passion they willingly share.

Presumably because Tristan is the heroic figure in this
romance, Thomas does not compare Mark directly to
Arthur. The poet suggests that Mark plays Arthur's role,
for in this version Mark is king of all England, but it is
Tristan who is shaped in the image of Arthur. It is Tristan
who fights the enormous nephew of Orgillos, the giant

whom Arthur himself had slain. Tristan no longer needs Arthur's help, as he does in Eilhart's poem, but equals him, assuming his heritage in his roles of ideal protector and lover.

God is on the lovers' side, and so Thomas suppresses the figure of Ogrin. In the ordeal scene Isolt safely carries the red-hot iron, "and God in his gentle mercy granted her sweet vindication and reconciliation and concord with the king, her lord and husband, with abundant love, honor, and esteem."[9] Thus, God protects Tristan and Isolt and justifies the laws of their worldly love.

Friedrich Naumann explains courtly culture in these words: "Man bejaht die Welt, die man eigentlich nicht bejahen sollte. Man bejaht die Welt mit einer Schambewegung. Diese gezähmte, zögernde, verhüllte Weltbejahung des Mittelalters nennen wir höfische Kultur."[10] Thomas's lovers belong to the courtly world. Mark's legal rights are of no value when compared to those of reciprocal love. And so he appears as a weak, pathetic figure, a nonentity who suffers and causes others to suffer. He is merely an obstacle to the fulfillment of Tristan's and Isolt's love, a catalyst causing their death.

Thomas's work clearly belongs within the ranks of courtly literature. It exalts love, presents love's psychology, and is directed to lovers. These two key words, love and psychology, make clear that Thomas addresses himself as much to the emotion as to the intellect of his audience.

Gottfried von Strassburg does not write for all lovers; he writes only for the *edelen herzen* (noble hearts, v. 47, p. 42), those who strive to reach the very essence of love which

Gottfried describes in the well-known formula "I have another world in mind which together in one heart bears its
bitter-sweet, its dear sorrow, its heart's joy, its love's pain,
its dear life, its sorrowful death, its dear death, its sorrowful life" (vv. 58–63, p. 42).

Tristan and Isolt find their way to the world of the *edelen
herzen* when they drink the love potion. In opposition to
courtly lovers who look for personal satisfaction only—in
this version the concept of courtliness thus carries with it
a negative connotation—Tristan and Isolt serve Love. It is
here that a religious element enters the romance. One
might say that the love potion is for Tristan and Isolt what
grace is for the Christian saint.[11] Eilhart's *unsêlig trang*
(cursed drink, v. 9489[12]) has become a blessed drink. Mark
does not take part in this world of the noble hearts, and
therefore he cannot partake of the love potion.[13]

Immediately after Tristan and Isolt have acknowledged
their love and accepted it as constituting their true being
by surrendering to one another, the poet inserts a "discourse on Love" (vv. 12187–361, pp. 202–4), where he
interprets Tristan's and Isolt's reciprocal feeling, opposing
it to the love of the world, the pursuit of happiness. He
lets us understand that for Tristan and Isolt physical love
is the expression of their deep feeling, religiously speaking, a sacrament.[14] For Mark, the courtly lover, physical
love is not a means but an end. He does not recognize the
truth Isolt embodies. Lying with Brangaene and Isolt, "he
found gold and brass in either" (vv. 12674–75, p. 208). He
therefore is not willing to fight for his wife. When Gandin
insists on taking Isolt with him, Mark looks for someone
to defend her. Because of Gandin's strength, nobody vol-

unteers, "nor was Mark willing to fight for Isolde in person" (vv. 13253–54, p. 216).[15] What Mark looks for in love is possession not devotion.

Thus he cannot decide whether he should believe Isolt innocent or guilty. He submits to the counsel of his courtiers and tries to force his wife into betraying herself. But he is convinced of the love between Tristan and Isolt not through any of the tricks his counselors devise, but through his own observation: he sees their love in Isolt's eyes—not Tristan's—another indication of the courtly, possessive character of his love. "It was death to his reason that his darling Isolde should love any man but himself" (vv. 16521–24, p. 258). His love turns to jealousy and anger, and he bans Tristan and Isolt. How courtly his love is, in the positive sense of the word, becomes clear when we hear him say that he loves them too much to want to take vengeance: "Take each other by the hand and leave my court and country. If I am to be wronged by you I wish neither to see nor hear it" (vv. 16607–10, p. 259), and so he grants Tristan and Isolt the happiest time of their lives. His generosity, however, cannot be compared to that of the king at the end of Eilhart's poem, for he is blind to the truth and is moved by self-pity. This is why Gottfried's Mark appears less tragic than pathetic.

In the love-cave scene Tristan and Isolt reach union with the summum bonum. It is a realm closed off, where Mark can find no entrance. Through the window he sees Isolt— he scarcely looks at Tristan—and her beauty makes his passion return with the same intensity as before. As in Thomas's version of the story, he wants to protect her from the sun, but he does not use his glove, the sign of her dependence on him within courtly society: if she returns to him it will be because she wants to not because she has to. Blocking out the sun, Mark takes honor away from the lovers, for Gottfried had told us earlier that the sun represented "that blessed radiance, Honour, dearest of all luminaries" (vv. 17071–72, p. 265), the honor of divine love, not that of courtly society. On the contrary, Mark restores worldly honor to the lovers when he calls them back. Gottfried underlines the precariousness of Mark's relationship with Isolt by saying: "Mark was happy once more. For his happiness he again had in his wife Isolde all that his heart desired—not in honour, but materially" (vv. 17727–31, pp. 274–75), and he shows his contempt for such a love in his long digression on jealous husbands.

It is in fact Mark's jealous suspicion that makes him surprise Tristan and Isolt and causes his agony. The final judgment of Mark is pronounced, ironically, by his counselors: "You hate your honour and your wife, but most of all yourself" (vv. 18389–90, p. 282). Since Mark's situation springs from his concern for himself, it is diametrically opposed to that of Tristan.

But what might have become of this hatred after Tristan's and Isolt's death? Learning that they had died for one another, would Mark not have recognized that he would not have been capable of giving up his life for his wife's sake? Would he not have realized that Tristan and Isolt were drawn together by a feeling much stronger than his love had ever been? Would he not have acknowledged the truth known to the *edelen herzen*? Such an ending seems possible when we consider Mark's words at the banishment scene: "Since I can read it in the pair of you that, in defiance of my will, you love and have loved each other more than me, then be with one another as you please" (vv. 16596–601, p. 259). De Boor's interpretation takes the same direction. He compares Mark to the pagan king of the saint legend who causes the martyr's death only to recognize his own mistake and to convert to the true religion.[16]

Such an ending would be comparable to that of Eilhart's poem insofar as Mark understands that he has fought against a power superior to his own, but it would be different from that of Eilhart, because it would not be tragic. All through the story Mark is clearly at fault for not recognizing what he sees. He is not a victim of fate but of his self-centered outlook on life. At best he is a pathetic figure, at worst a villain intent on destroying the truth.

Arthur is mentioned only once in this text. Gottfried sets the *Minnegrotte* apart from the Round Table: "Their company of two was so ample a crowd for this pair that good King Arthur never held a feast in any of his palaces that gave keener pleasure or delight" (vv. 16863–67, p. 263). Tristan is not Arthur's heir, but surpasses his splendor. Mark, on the other hand, does not reach Arthur's glory. Arthur outdoes him then, but on a material level, not on a spiritual one.

The role of God has troubled many scholars.[17] In the ordeal scene Gottfried says: "Thus it was made manifest and confirmed to all the world that Christ in His great virtue is pliant as a windblown sleeve" (vv. 15737–40, p. 248). But what does this passage mean if not that Gottfried mocks the attitudes of the church? After all, it is the ecclesiastical establishment that devises the ordeal; and not

God but courtly society is deceived by the wording of the oath. Gottfried never lets us know where God stands, perhaps because in his work love takes God's place.[18]

Like Thomas's poem, Gottfried's *Tristan* affects the reader's emotions and demands that he reflect on its content. It requires, however, a more sophisticated audience capable of grasping new concepts and recognizing subtleties of which Thomas never dreamed. In other words, Gottfried's poem is written for an elite courtly public.

The French prose romance, on the other hand, aims at entertaining the bourgeoisie as well as the nobility. The prologue states that the Tristan legend "would be a thing that poor and rich alike would very much enjoy, as long as they were willing to hear and listen to the beautiful adventures that are so very pleasing" (p. 1). Speaking of the various episodes Eugène Vinaver states: "Leur intérêt n'est plus dans les idées qu'ils illustrent; il réside dans les intrigues et les événements qu'ils racontent."[19] Psychological intricacies are not in the foreground of the story, but this does not mean that there is no moral judgment; it is just an extremely simple one. Basically, the court of Arthur is good, and Mark, Andret, and most of the Cornish are bad (Tristan and Dinas are laudable exceptions). Dinadan, a brave Arthurian knight whom we respect for his independent and logical thought, says about Arthur's court: "The good who come there leave better, but whoever comes there bad and evil . . . and of wicked birth and wicked nature, cannot in any way change his being, just as copper cannot become gold or lead silver" (p. 113).[20] But "King Mark . . . would have appeared a worthy man and a valiant and wise prince, if he did not have a villainous face" (pp. 123–24).

The reader knows immediately what to think of Mark, whose first noteworthy deed in the romance is to kill his brother for no other reason than a well-deserved rebuke. The king uses Tristan when he needs a strong knight, as in the Morolt episode (interestingly enough, Morolt is a knight of the Round Table), but tries to destroy him at all other times. This is the only version where the animosity between uncle and nephew is established before Isolt is mentioned. Thus, Mark sends Tristan to Ireland not so much to fetch Isolt as in the hope that the Irish will kill the young knight. The king is as subject to his love for Isolt as in the versions by Thomas and Gottfried, but because of his unworthiness he does not earn our sympathy. Nor will the reader take his side when, obviously afraid of meeting his nephew face to face, he abducts Isolt twice from the protection of Tristan, who happens to be absent.

Mark's vilest deed is to ban Tristan from Cornwall, for this injustice toward his nephew contributes to the demise of Arthur's reign, a catastrophe for which Tristan acts as a catalyst since he undermines the Arthurian moral system by bringing out the worst in Arthur's knights. Gawain's first dishonorable deed is to threaten a damsel with death unless she tells him who her companion is, and that companion is Tristan.[21] Lancelot rewards Tristan's service with his friendship, but he is debased by it. For Lancelot, who had treated the affair with Guenevere with the utmost secrecy (cf. p. 79), now is linked to Tristan, who openly rebels against Mark, his king, and carries on a flagrant affair with Isolt, his queen. Under such circumstances, how can the knights of the Round Table hope to defend a moral system that is based on trust? How can they reach the Grail when their foremost representative is Lancelot?

But Mark influences the fate of Arthur's court directly as well. Twice he comes to Logres. The first time, he wants to kill Tristan. He splits the head of one of his own knights who does not agree with his plan and then successfully defends himself in single combat, taking advantage of his position as king (which exempts him from the obligation of swearing an oath on his innocence). He thereby all but destroys the moral system Arthur had constructed.

Mark returns, now intent on killing King Arthur, whose best knights are on the Grail quest. He succeeds in wounding Arthur dangerously, but he is defeated by Galahad, a representative not of Arthur's worldly kingdom but of God's spiritual reign. The Arthurian system has lost its balance. Arthur's knights, among them Tristan, the emissary of Mark, fail to attain the values Galahad serves and cannot even defend their king. There is nothing to fill this void. Mark has given the death blow to the Arthurian dream. It is no coincidence that Arthur at the same time learns of the disastrous outcome of the Grail quest and Tristan's death.

Tristan is not granted a heroic death but is killed by a poisoned lance that Mark, the vilest of all persons, treacherously thrusts at him. It is true that Mark later repents of this murder, but this repentance only underscores the despicability of his action.[22]

Without Mark's actions, Tristan could have been an

exemplary knight, better even than Lancelot. As it is, Mark's lack of honor debases Tristan and contributes to the destruction of Arthur's kingdom. He is a villain who ruins all.

In conclusion, Eilhart's poem glorifies feudal law and order. The story line is simple. Outside of the potion no motive is explained in detail. The text addresses itself to our emotions. Mark is a servant of God; morally he surpasses Arthur. He is good, a victim of fate and a hero in facing reality.

Thomas concerns himself with the suffering of unhappy lovers. The plot does not oppose right and wrong but instead presents the effects of love on unhappy lovers in different situations. The poem tells not only what happened but why. It addresses itself to our emotions as well as to our understanding. Mark does not understand God's will; he equals Arthur, but only in his feudal position. He is an unhappy lover who would like to do what is right, but who is too weak to accomplish anything. He loses himself, a victim of his longing for a love that cannot be.

Gottfried introduces a new concept by opposing generous to selfish love. He lets us know not only what happened and why but also what it means. The text speaks to our emotions, our understanding, and our judgment. Mark opposes love, which in this poem takes the place of God; he is inferior to Arthur, even on a material level. He is a selfish lover, a victim of his egoism. If indeed Gottfried meant to end the romance as we have suggested, the king would recognize his flaw, and thus go through the same learning process as the reader.

The author of the *Prose Tristan* is less concerned with ethos or psychology than with interlacing the various story lines. The characters are defined just enough to make their conduct believable. The text addresses itself primarily to our sense of plausibility. Mark opposes God's spiritual reign as well as Arthur's worldly kingdom. He is a villain.

The uncourtly versions of Eilhart and the *Prose Tristan* present a relatively simple form of ethos, of reader manipulation, and of character portrayal. It is the courtly versions of Thomas and Gottfried that really define the ethos, address the whole psychological being of their reader, and that present complex characters who are neither good nor bad but fundamentally human. Might the confluence of these three qualities be one of the properties of courtly narrative literature?

NOTES

1. Joan Ferrante, *The Conflict of Love and Honor: The Medieval Tristan Legend in France, Germany and Italy*, De Proprietatibus Litterarum, Series Practica, no. 78 (The Hague: Mouton, 1973).

2. Franz Lichtenstein, ed., *Eilhart von Oberge*, Quellen und Forschungen zur Sprach- und Kulturgeschichte der germanischen Völker, no. 19 (Strassburg: Karl J. Trübner, 1877); Thomas, *Les Fragments du Roman de Tristan*, ed. Bartina H. Wind, Textes Littéraires Français, no. 92 (Geneva: Droz, 1960); Gottfried von Strassburg, *Tristan*, ed. Reinhold Bechstein, 5th ed. (Leipzig: Brockhaus, 1930); E. Löseth, ed., *Le Roman de Tristan, Le Roman de Palamède et La Compilation de Rusticien de Pise: Analyse critique d'après les manuscrits de Paris* (Paris, 1891; rpt. New York: Burt Franklin, 1970).

For Eilhart's text, I quote *Eilhart von Oberge's Tristrant*, trans. J. W. Thomas (Lincoln: University of Nebraska Press, 1978).

For the texts of Thomas and Gottfried, I quote Gottfried von Strassburg, *Tristan with the Tristan of Thomas*, trans. A. T. Hatto (Baltimore: Penguin, 1960). All other translations are mine. Each quotation is followed by a verse reference to the original text or a page reference for the *Prose Tristan* and, for Eilhart, Thomas, and Gottfried, a page reference to the respective translation.

3. Jean Marx, "Observations sur un épisode de la légende de Tristan," in *Recueil de travaux offert à M. Clovis Brunel* (Paris: Société de l'Ecole des Chartes, 1955), pp. 265–73. See as well Eugène Vinaver's answer to Marx in *A La Recherche d'une poétique médiévale* (Paris: Nizet, 1970), pp. 92–94.

4. Ferrante, p. 51.

5. This is my understanding of "sô muste mich got hônen." J. W. Thomas translates the verse as "may God scorn me" (p. 103).

6. Because Thomas's version of this scene is not extant, I am basing my observations on Brother Robert's translation of his text. The passage alluded to can be found in *The Saga of Tristan and Isönd*, trans. Paul Schach (Lincoln: University of Nebraska Press, 1973), p. 72.

7. Ibid., p. 103.

8. I have altered Hatto's translation of "Huntage avenir vus en deit / Quant tuz ses bons li cunsentez" (vv. 392–93), which he renders as "dishonour is bound to overtake you if you consent to all her wishes." In her edition, Bartina H. Wind translates "Que fere li osissez senblant" (v. 402) as "de lui montrer ce que vous pensez d'elle" (to show her what you think of her; p. 102n).

9. Schach translation, p. 94.

10. Friedrich Naumann, "Hohe Minne," *Zeitschrift für Deutschkunde* 39 (1925): 81–91, at p. 81. (One assents to the world, to which one should actually not assent. One assents to the world with some embarrassment. This medieval assent to the world, restrained, hesitant, covert, is what we call courtly culture.)

11. This interpretaticn differs fundamentally from that of W. T. H. Jackson, "Gottfried von Straussburg," in *Arthurian Literature in the Middle Ages: A Collaborative History*, ed. Roger Sherman Loomis (Oxford: Clarendon Press, 1959), pp. 145–56, who believes that the potion "hands them [Tristan and Isolt] over to the tyranny of the senses, and this tyranny is so powerful that it brushes from its path all considerations of honour and loyalty. . . . So strong is it, indeed, that the ultimate sin is committed in its name, when the oath before God is reduced to a mockery by a crude piece of deception" (p. 153).

12. J. W. Thomas translates the adjective as "fatal" (p. 155).

13. Gottfried underlines this difference from Thomas: "No, none of that philtre remained. Brangane had thrown it into the sea" (vv. 12659–60, p. 208).

14. Again, this interpretation differs from that of W. T. H. Jackson: "The love of Tristan and Isolt is a mystic love in human terms. Its purer aspects were subjected through drinking the potion to the devil of sensual passion. Only by death can their love be freed from this snare and the 'love-death' means that the lovers can be reunited in mystic love, freed from all grossness and carnal attraction" (p. 154).

15. It is Tristan who brings her back. Joan Ferrante claims that "the point is to diminish Mark's legal, and therefore to some extent, his moral claims to Isolt, and so strengthen Tristan's in contrast" (p. 45). However, since Mark and Tristan operate on two different levels, Isolt belongs to Tristan and there is no need for him to strengthen his position. Tristan's saving Isolt is an effect of the truth they both represent, not an attempt to establish that truth. On the other hand, Mark's action does not mean that because of his cowardice he no longer has a legal right to his wife. By the same reasoning he would have lost his claim to his kingdom by not doing battle with the Morolt.

16. Helmut de Boor, "Die Grundauffassung von Gottfrieds Tristan," *Deutsche Vierteljahresschrift* 18 (1940): 262–306; rpt. in *Gottfried von Strassburg*, ed. Alois Wolf, Wege der Forschung,

no. 320 (Darmstadt: Wissenschaftliche Buchgesellschaft, 1973), pp. 25–73, at p. 68.

17. For a bibliography, see Ferrante, pp. 52–53n.

18. Cf. de Boor, pp. 68–73, where he analyzes the reasons for the "organic mistake" in Gottfried's poem.

19. Eugène Vinaver, *Etudes sur le Tristan en Prose* (Paris: Champion, 1925), p. 13. (Their interest no longer lies in the ideas they exemplify but in the intrigues and events they recount.)

20. For an assessment of Dinadan's character and role in the *Prose Tristan*, see Vinaver, *Etudes*, pp. 91–98.

21. Only once before is there an allusion to Gawain's worthless character. Significantly, it is Tristan who makes the remark (p. 28).

22. Emmanuèle Baumgartner, *Le "Tristan en Prose": Essai d'interprétation d'un roman médiéval*, Publications Romanes et Françaises, no. 133 (Geneva: Droz, 1975), comments: "Sincèrement épris d'Iseut, par moments accessible à la pitié et au repentir, Marc reste, en dépit de tout l'odieux de sa conduite, un être humain et non un traître de mélodrame" (p. 230). (Sincerely in love with Isolt, at times capable of pity and repentance, Mark remains, in spite of his detestable conduct, a human being and not a traitor of melodrama.)

III

Twelfth-Century
Changes

The *Sen* of
Chrétien de Troyes's *Joie de la Cort*

TERENCE SCULLY

One problem that any reader of the works of Chrétien de Troyes must settle for himself is whether to attempt to read "meaning" into the adventures that Chrétien's heroes are made to undergo. Have the episodes been invented in order to tell the audience something about the meaning of the plot and the hero's role in it, or do they exist merely as demonstrations of the hero's chivalric prowess and nobility?

Chrétien's imagination seems remarkably rich; the precision of many adventures is surprising. It is perplexing how he insists upon a whole series of details as if they were important to the value or significance of the adventure. An instance might be Yvain's adventure of the *château de pesme aventure*, with its three-hundred captive maidens sent as ransom by the seventeen-year-old king of the Isle as Pucelles and now laboring for two sons of a *netun*. An even more bizarre assemblage of details is found in the last adventure to which Erec is exposed: a garden with an invisible wall contains medicinal herbs, a bellicose knight, a recumbent lady, a horn, and a number of impaled heads!

Faced so often with such precise nonsense,[1] the reader wonders what guided Chrétien's imagination. He may properly ask whether such bizarre scenes might reveal what the author intended each work as a whole to be

about. The modern reader might try doing what any edu-
cated person in Chrétien's audience would have done: to
assume that the story might be an allegory with a subsidi-
ary sense that could be uncovered by systematic exegesis.
It would be useful to examine closely the final adventure
in *Erec et Enide* and to seek an allegorical interpretation that
might clarify the *sen* of the romance.

In *Erec et Enide* the peculiar final adventure concludes a
whole sequence of adventures that Erec has voluntarily
undertaken and is the longest and most developed of them.
It immediately precedes the concluding scenes of the romance. We might reasonably expect this episode to have
been called, like the last one in *Yvain*, the "supreme adventure," or the "most fearsome test," or the "ultimate combat," or something suggesting the culmination in Erec's
search. Instead, the episode is called merely *la Joie de la
Cort*. It is so named repeatedly, as if to emphasize its special significance as a clue to this strange adventure, and
perhaps to the sense of the whole romance.

Several critics have attempted to show that this material has not been gratuitously invented by Chrétien but
adapted with some degree of deliberateness from certain
sources. For Emmanuel Philippot, the *Joie de la Cort* was
inspired by the novel *Le Bel inconnu* and its English treatment *Libeaus Desconus*. In 1936 Helaine Newstead proposed that "the title [*Joie de la Cort*] correctly describes the
joy that follows the acquisition or restoration of the horn
of plenty," reading *cor* for *cort* and making a connection
with the Celtic mythological figure of Bran. R. S. Loomis
similarly held that "almost every feature [of the *Joie de la
Cort*] can be accounted for by the coalescence of two fa-

mous themes—the visit to the castle of Bran and the release of Mabon from captivity." William A. Nitze expressed the opinion that Chrétien intended *Erec* as an "epithalamium or wedding romance" in which Chrétien was defending, as elsewhere, his ideal of a perfect, equally balanced marriage, with the *Joie de la Cort* condemning *accidia*—"sloth," or, quoting Tennyson, "uxoriousness." According to Jean Frappier, all the adventures in Erec's second quest spring from Erec's need to demonstrate his prowess again and to test Enide's love for him.[2]

And most recently, D. Kelly has proposed that the *sen* of the *bele conjointure* of *Erec* might be understood, with other works of Chrétien, as a sort of quest to demonstrate that "la valeur du chevalier provient au fond du seul amour qu'il porte à son amie." His particular interpretation seems, however, to spring primarily from a view of Enide as a misunderstanding, unappreciative wife. Kelly is quite right in insisting that we should try to understand what Chrétien wanted to say before seeking the sources he may have made use of. There is, it seems to me, something largely futile about efforts to "explain" an author of any period solely by showing how other writers used similar material. Kelly recognizes one of the problems: "La quête d'Erec est un peu plus complexe [than Yvain's], puisque sa fin ne coïncide pas avec celle du roman, et la réconciliation avec Enide précède d'autres aventures subies au cours de retour."[3]

According to this interpretation, the climax of the poem in which husband and wife have demonstrated their respective worth would occur sometime before the *Joie de la Cort* episode. "Chrétien insiste sur l'erreur commise par Enide

en donnant créance aux critiques de compagnons d'Erec
et en doutant de la valeur de son mari; elle se rend compte
de cette erreur dès les premières victoires d'Erec et ne cesse
désormais de se reprocher sa *parole*" (p. 353). The reader
consequently would wonder why Chrétien continued the
series of adventures with Erec's second meeting with
Guivret le Petit, and with the *Joie de la Cort*. Chrétien
seems not too concerned with proportion, as Erec continues to seek yet a further adventure. The *Joie de la Cort*
seems unnecessary to prove Erec's chivalric valor; nor
does it add to our appreciation of Enide's fidelity.

I suspect that, rather than beginning with Enide's sigh
and subsequent expressions of guilt, we should first consider the final adventure and look to it to clarify the sense
of the quest in *Erec*.

Philippot (p. 289) admitted that the parallels he perceived between the *Joie de la Cort* and *Le Bel inconnu* were
not entirely sufficient to "explain" Chrétien's version of
the episode. "Une dernière obscurité subsiste: le titre seul
de 'la Joie de la Cour' est une énigme, la plus déconcer-
tante, pour le lecteur." He did, however, see a possible
source for the name in the prose *Tristan*, where Lancelot's
isle is called the "Ile de la Joie"; but beyond that somewhat
doubtful parallel in name, the modern reader still has little
indication why Chrétien used the episode or named it as
he did. These are, I think, the two most difficult problems:
what is the sense of the *Joie de la Cort*, and how does it fit
into *Erec et Enide*?

What is immediately striking about Chrétien's text is his
insistence upon the name of the adventure even more than

upon its nature. When interrogating Guivret le Petit about it, Erec asks

> "De l'avanture vos apel
> Que seulemant le nom me dites,
> et del sorplus soiez toz quites." ★
>   [5408–10]⁴

Guivret willingly responds:

> "L'avanture, ce vos plevis,
> la Joie de la Cort a non." †
>   [5416–17]

Even stranger than this emphasis upon the name is Erec's delight at hearing the name and his declaration that this is precisely what he has been looking for since he set forth with Enide on his quest:

> "Dex! an joie n'a se bien non,
> fet Erec; ce vois je querant. . . .
> Rien ne me porroit retenir
> que je n'aille querre la Joie." ‡ ⁵
>   [5418–19, 5424–25]

The word *joie* seems to designate more than just the promised adventure about which Erec knows nothing yet, but whose *joie* he prizes above all, as what one might call a chief good. Is Erec meant to be so self-seeking that he is pursuing absolute pleasure throughout the world, as a sort of twelfth-century hedonist? This is hard to believe. And

★ "I appeal to you concerning the adventure that you tell me just the name of it, and I'll not insist upon the rest."
† "The adventure, upon my word, is called 'the Joy of the Court.'"
‡ "God! there can be nothing but good in joy," says Erec; "I go to seek it. . . . Nothing could restrain me from going to seek the Joy."

yet that this *joie* is a *thing* in Chrétien's mind is confirmed repeatedly, for Erec speaks of it as something to be obtained, won, acquired, or shared in.

Erec says to King Evrain:

> "La Joie de la Cort demant,
> car nule rien tant ne covoit.
> Donez la moi, que que ce soit,
> se vos an estes posteïs." ★
>   [5556–59]

And the King replies:

> "Vos l'avroiz ancontre mon pois,
> la Joie que vos requerez" †
>   [5610–11]

but goes on to wish:

> ". . . Dex, si con je le desir,
> vos an doint a joie partir." ‡
>   [5619–20]

The people pity Erec:

> "Chevaliers, Joie t'a traï,
> ceste que tu cuides conquerre,
> mes ta mort et ton duel vas querre." ★
>   [5656–58]

Chrétien even speaks of the birds in the garden

★ "I ask you for 'the Joy of the Court,' for I covet nothing else so much. Grant it to me, whatever it be, if you are in control of it."
† "You are acting against my will. You shall have the Joy which you desire."
‡ "May God, as I desire, grant you to share in Joy."
★ "Oh knight, the Joy that thou wishest to win has betrayed thee, and thou goest to win but grief and death."

> qui la Joie li presantoient,
> la chose a coi il plus baoit. †
>
> [5722–23]

In medieval literature when troubadours or trouvères sang of *joie* the audience immediately understood the word to designate the perfect pleasure of good love; I think this is what Chrétien intended, and expected, his audience to understand. The *joie* here is a love to be sought and possessed, but it is a particular type of *joie*, since it is *de la cort*. This qualification is of the greatest importance because a distinction was made in twelfth-century courtly convention between what might be called natural or purely sensual love and that refined code of amorous behavior worked out in the courts of southern France and known today as courtly love. What Chrétien would be referring to here is a *joie* more perfect than that in which our hero Erec, with natural gusto, indulged immediately following his marriage.[6] This last and greatest adventure promises rather to put him in possession of the only ideal *joie*, the *joie de la cort*, which for Chrétien would be the amorous state of mind and inspiration approved by *courtoisie*.

The courtly joy[7] that Erec has been seeking since the beginning of his odyssey cannot be had easily. Winning courtly *joie* demands an arduous and perilous struggle which, we are constantly reminded, has already killed many otherwise worthy men who had sought to possess it.

> "Cist chevaliers, qui par ci passe,
> vient a la Joie de la Cort.

† . . . which put him in mind of his Joy—the thing he most was longing for.

Dolant en iert einz qu'il s'an tort:
onques nus ne vint d'autre terre
la Joie de la Cort requerre
qu'il n'i eüst honte et domage
et n'i leissast la teste an gage."

. . . .

"Et sachiez bien que j'ai veüz
mainz prodomes et receüz,
qui ceste Joie demanderent."‡
[5462–68, 5579–81]

The name of the adventure is indeed bizarre unless it denotes something valuable which by its nature may cause suffering and death to those who pursue it.

"Ceste Joie, Dex la Maudie,
que tant preudome i sont ocis.
Hui an cest jor fera le pis
que onques mes feïst sanz dote."★
[5660–63]

"Feites voz genz arriere trere,
car la Joie vanra par tans,
qui vos fera dolant, ce pans."†
[5774–76]

Surely what Chrétien is talking about here is the agony of *fin' amors*. The field of stakes, with the skulls of those

‡"This knight, who is passing, is on his way to the 'Joy of the Court.' He will be sorry before he returns; no one ever came from another land to claim the 'Joy of the Court' who did not receive shame and harm, and leave his head there as a forfeit. . . . And know well that I have seen many a man ruined who solicited this Joy."
★"God curse this Joy! which has been the death of so many gentlemen. Today it will wreak the worst woe that it has ever yet wrought."
†"Have your men withdraw; for 'the Joy' will soon arrive, and will make you sorry, I suspect."

who have failed the test, is reminiscent of the valley of amorous death which still turns up in narrative poems in the fifteenth century.[8] Courtly *joie* demands a suffering such as even valiant men cannot survive, and its requirements may, as with Yvain, lead even to a loss of sanity. King Evrain gives Erec fair warning about this danger:

> "Ceste chose est molt dolereuse,
> Car dolant a fet maint prodome.
> Vos meïsmes a la parsome
> an seroiz morz et afolez."‡
>
> [5562–65]

The man who undertakes this *joie* may even regret doing so because the struggle might in the end be too costly:

> "Einz que demain soit aseri,
> poez ausi de vos atandre,
> se la Joie volez anprandre,
> que vos l'avroiz, mes bien vos poist.
> C'est une chose qui vos loist
> a repantir et a retraire,
> se vos volez vostre preu faire."★
>
> [5584–90]

But the convention held that out of this total devotion to the lady's service will flow the primary qualities of the courtly lover, especially *prix* and *honor*. It is highly revealing that precisely these terms of *prix* and *honor* recur here,

‡"This is a very parlous thing, which has caused sorrow to many a worthy man; you yourself will eventually be killed and undone if you will not heed my counsel."
★"Before tomorrow's evening come you may expect a like reward. If you wish to strive for the Joy, you shall do so, though it grieve me sore. It is something from which you are free to retreat and draw back if you wish to work your welfare."

designating the rewards that Erec is expecting to win in the
Joie de la Cort. If Erec is largely ignorant of what awaits
him in the adventure, he does anticipate what the rewards
will be. As the King says of Erec's determination to try for
the *Joie*,

> "De rien nule ne me mervoil,
> se vos querez enor et pris."†
> [5575–76]

And again Chrétien, through King Evrain, stresses the
supreme nature of this adventure, in another instance
where I suspect Chrétien intends *joie* to be understood as
Joie:

> ". . . Des or estes an fiance
> d'avoir quanque vos covoitiez;
> se vos a joie an esploitiez,
> conquise avroiz si grant enor
> onques hom ne conquist graignor."‡
> [5614–18]

The blowing of the horn, signaling total success in the
adventure, will mark too the acquisition of *prix* and *honor*.

> "Del cor ne vos dirai je plus,
> fors c'onques soner nel pot nus;
> mes cil qui soner le porra,
> et son pris et s'enor fera
> devant toz ces de ma contree."★
> [5765–69]

† "I am not at all surprised that you desire honour and fame."
‡ "But now be assured that you shall have what you desire. If you come
out of it happily, you will have won such great honour that never did
man win greater."
★ "I will tell you nothing of the horn; but never has anyone been able

Maboagrain himself assures Erec of the exalted nature of his achievement:

> "... Sachiez bien, n'est pas petite
> l'enors que vos avez conquise."†
>   [6066–67]

The adventure of the *Joie de la Cort* is very carefully not set in the courtyard of some fantastic castle or in a clearing of a forest, where one might reasonably expect a formally disposed combat to take place, but rather in the conventional spring garden, the *vergier*, a commonplace in the courtly lyric though not usually the setting for a battle to the death. We find here all of the standard elements of the twelfth-century courtly Garden of Eden, the *locus amoenus*: the grounds are eternally graced by flowers and fruit and all sorts of agreeable songbirds. It is precisely these birds that welcome Erec, armed for combat, into the garden and, most peculiarly, "manifest" the *Joie* to him.

> Erec aloit, lance sor fautre,
> par mi le vergier chevauchant,
> qui molt se delitoit el chant
> des oisiax qui leanz chantoient,
> qui la Joie le presantoient,
> la chose a coi il plus baoit. ‡
>   [5718–23]

---

to blow it. However, he who shall succeed in blowing it—his fame and honour will grow until it distance all those of my country."

†"Be assured that it is no small honour which you have gained."

‡Erec went riding, lance in rest, into the middle of the garden, greatly delighting in the song of the birds which were singing there; they put him in mind of his Joy—the thing he most was longing for.

They behave in much the same way as the birds in the courtly lyric do when they urge the poet to discover the *joie* of true love.

An unusual feature within this garden of *joie*—apart from the rows of stakes and heads—is the presence of great numbers of medicinal plants.

> Et terre, tant com ele dure,
> ne port espice ne mecine,
> qui vaille a nule medecine,
> que iluec n'i eüst planté,
> s'an i avoit a grant planté.★
> [5710–14]

Their inclusion there among the birds, flowers, and fruit can most easily be understood as a further topos of courtly love, in which the lady is regarded as a doctor for the afflicted lover, and love provides, paradoxically, a remedy for the suffering it causes. Without this conventional interpretation the audience would be hard put, I believe, to understand why Chrétien had put all these herbal remedies in this luxuriant garden where so many worthy men had died.

The nature of the enclosure around the strange garden must also have been recognizable to the twelfth-century audience. Even though, as Kelly (pp. 332–34) has pointed out, Chrétien rarely uses the supernatural or marvelous, he does so in this most important adventure in *Erec*. The allegory remains to be expounded: why is the marvelous

---

★ And the earth, however far it stretch, bears no spice or root of use in making medicine, but it had been planted there, and was to be found in abundance.

garden-cum-combat ground isolated? Why can its peculiar, abundant fruit be enjoyed only there; why can no one
remove it and enjoy it outside?

> Et li fruiz avoit tel eür
> que leanz se lessoit mangier,
> mes au porter hors fet dongier;
> car qui point an volsist porter
> ne s'an seüst ja mes raler,
> car a l'issue ne venist
> tant qu'an son leu le remeïst†
>
> [5698–704]

The answer that immediately suggests itself is that what
is produced within this garden, what goes on there, the
struggles, the suffering, and the eventual pleasures are all
exclusive to that area: this *hortus conclusus* constitutes a
world apart, constructed quite differently from the outside
world. It is an "other world" of love such as was commonly conceived by medieval writers. For Guillaume de
Lorris the wall serves to exclude from his ideal world all
that is undesirable.[9] But why, then, in *Erec*, the remarkable wall of air which forms just as solid a barrier as that
in the *Roman de la Rose*? In fact Chrétien's wall is even
more solid because the wall is like one of iron:

> El vergier n'avoit an viron
> mur ne paliz, se de l'air non;
> mes de l'air est de totes parz

---

† And the fruit was of such a nature that it could be eaten inside; the
danger consisted in carrying it out; for whoever should wish to carry
out a little would never be able to find the gate, and never could issue
from the garden until he had restored the fruit to its place.

par nigromance clos li jarz,
si que riens antrer n'i pooit
se par un seul leu n'i antroit,
ne que s'il fust toz clos de fer. ‡
[5689–95]

Chrétien's point seems to be that this wall of air is transparent. Anyone on the outside can see in and think that he could enter into the bliss of this Eden; but he cannot. Despite appearances, these *are* different worlds; only the very select qualify to seek the mysterious pleasure of the *Joie*. The explanation that springs to mind is that Chrétien wanted to represent not a physical wall but rather a moral, even spiritual one which could represent the absolute (although invisible) social, cultural, and ethical barrier that sets the insiders apart from the outsiders.[10] Chrétien could very well be thinking of the new convention of courtly love which insisted upon the initiation of the select few to certain rules of behavior and the acceptance of almost occult tenets about the effects of love. Into this closed mystical world Erec steps in the painful struggle to win *Joie*.

The battle itself is the central event in the adventure, yet the motives for it are perhaps the strangest of Chrétien's inventions. Erec enters the garden alone and spies a silver bed with a golden sheet and a beautiful lady sitting upon it. The scene is reminiscent of an Andrew Wyeth tableau in which the lady assumes certain symbolic qualities: her solitude seems to make her very largely an abstraction, perhaps representing womanhood as a whole. Without pause,

‡The garden had around it no wall or fence except of air, yet, by a spell, the garden was on all sides so shut in by the air that nothing could enter there any more than if the garden was enclosed in iron.

though with great temerity, Erec goes to sit beside her,
and this act triggers the confrontation with Maboagrain.

> Erec s'aproche cele part,
> qui de plus pres la vialt veoir;
> lez li s'ala Erec seoir.
> A *tant* ez vos un chevalier . . ..★
> [5844–47; my italics]

The giant's first words confirm what the action has already indicated: he considers himself mortally affronted
by Erec's boldness in sitting beside his lady.

> . . . "Vasax! Vasax!
> Fos estes, si ge soie sax,
> qui vers ma dameisele alez.
> Mien esciant, tant ne valez
> que vers li doiez aprochier.
> Vos conparroiz ancüi molt chier
> vostre folie, par ma teste.
> Estez arriers!"†   [5857–64]

This accusation "tant ne valez" amounts to a challenge,
and Erec accepts it as such, but the real basis for the ensu-
ing combat is the contention that Erec was unworthy of
approaching the perfectly beautiful lady. After a long and
exhausting battle, the defeated Maboagrain explains how
the "adventure" came into being. We learn that a blind
oath bound him to his lady, exclusively and uniquely, for
what she expected to be his whole lifetime.

★ Erec draws near to her, wishing to see her more closely, and goes to
sit beside her. Then behold, there comes a knight . . ..
† "Vassal, vassal! You are mad, upon my life, thus to approach my
damsel. I should say you are not worthy to draw near her. You will pay
dearly for your presumption, by my head! Stand back!"

"Ensi me cuida retenir
ma demeisele a lonc sejor;
. . . me cuida a delivre,
toz les jorz que j'eüsse a vivre,
avoec li tenir an prison. ‡
      [6040–41, 6045–47]

While the couple had known and loved one another since childhood, it was only from the time that he had been dubbed a knight—in the same *vergier*, on the occasion when he assumed his name, Maboagrain—that he realized the full extent of his obligation to his lady. It was then that, to use Chrétien's own term, he was caught in a "prison." Now that Maboagrain has been beaten, Erec can blow the horn, Maboagrain will be "desprisoné" (l. 6096) and "*lors commencera la Joie*" (l. 6097). There is a general rejoicing as people learn of Erec's victory and gather together.

The outcome of this battle is of momentous significance. Not only is Maboagrain freed from his vow, and the court of his uncle Evrain turned into the site of three-day festivity, but Erec has conquered something for himself and for everyone. Just what this is is never explained, yet it is consistently called *Joie*, and Chrétien seems to have thought this one word sufficient to make the sense of the episode clear. In overcoming Maboagrain and undoing the oath that controlled his life, Erec has managed to win *joie* for himself and for Evrain's court; in other words, he delivered true love to the courtly world. Maboagrain says to Erec about this *joie*:

‡"Thus my lady thought to detain me here for a long stay; . . . in this way she intended to keep me absolutely shut up with her all the days of my life."

"Tant longuemant l'ont atandue
que premiers lor sera randue
par vos, qui l'avez desresniée."★
[6075–77]

Erec himself had long yearned to know and possess this
joie—of which he was ignorant—as a supreme virtue; now
he bestows knowledge of it on all men by revealing it to
them with his joyous, mighty trumpet blast. The ideal of
true courtly love is now the property of all.

To understand what Chrétien conceives the essential element of courtly love to be brings us back to the shape of
the novel as a whole. Erec, by his chivalric prowess, won
Enide, but having done so he lost himself in carnal love.
His conjugal love became a passionate *druerie*—

a sa fame volt dosnoier,
si an fist s'amie et sa drue†
[2434–35]

—to which he became, unconsciously but banefully, so
bound that he forsook his chivalric obligations. This is bad
not because the couple have not made a good marriage but
simply because in their marriage they have not found good
love. It is on a quest for good love[11] that Erec must set
out. Erec's helpless, pitiful state then parallels that of
Maboagrain.

Both are held captive by their ladies, or rather by the
blameworthy vicissitudes of love which improperly seize

★"They have awaited it so long that now it will be granted them by
you who have won it by your fight."
†he spent his time making love to his wife, and made of her his sweet-
heart and his mistress

the whole man and restrain him forever. The quest in part freed Erec from the physical influence of Enide, and his adventures trace his progress toward a new independence of action. The first adventures reestablish the love of husband and wife on the firm base of mutual voluntary affection and respect.[12] With the final adventure, by freeing Maboagrain from his eternal promise, Erec secures the freedom of all lovers, married or not. It is only by the preservation of this vital freedom of will that the true *joie de la cort* can be known.

Enide, the unwillingly dominant spouse, is anxious as Erec passes from adventure to adventure; particularly in the concluding adventure she worries because she, like Erec, does not know what the adventure will entail, but also because she will not be able to accompany him any further. For the first time since their marriage they will be separated: he must go alone. His act of defeating whatever it is that constrains Maboagrain must be an independent act, in which he will be strengthened not by Enide's actual physical presence but by the intangible strength of her love. This is literally the *vertu* of the *joie de la cort*, a spiritual power.

> "Je ne puis plus ci arester,
> ne vos n'iroiz plus avoec moi,
> car avant mener ne vos doi,
> si con li rois l'a commandé."
> Lors la beise et comande a Dé,
> et ele i recomande lui;
> mes molt li torne a grant enui,
> quant ele nel siust et convoie
> tant qu'ele sache et qu'ele voie

quex avanture ce sera,
et comant il esploitera;
mes a remenoir li estuet,
car avant sivre ne le puet:
ele remaint triste et dolant. ‡
[5814–27]

Following Maboagrain's defeat, Enide's anxiety is echoed in the sorrow of his lady, who alone does not rejoice in the *Joie* after Erec has freed Maboagrain. It appears to her that she has now lost her lover; but Enide comforts her.

Molt fist Enyde que cortoise:
por ce que pansive la vit
et seule seoir sor le lit,
li prist talanz que ele iroit
a li, . . .
. . . por celi feire confort
a cui la Joie enuioit fort. ⋆
[6146–50, 6161–62]

Again we find the oxymoron of the "sorrowful joy" in the dismay that the *joie* may cause. As for Maboagrain's lady, she feared

‡ "I cannot longer tarry here, nor can you go along with me; for, as the King has ordered, I must not take you beyond this point." Then he kisses her and commends her to God, and she him. But she is much chagrined that she cannot follow and escort him, until she may learn and see what this adventure is to be, and how he will conduct himself. But since she must stay behind and cannot follow him, she remains sorrowful and grieving.

⋆ Enide acted graciously: because she saw her sitting pensive, alone on the couch, she felt moved to go and speak with her . . . to comfort her to whom the Joy brings great chagrin.

> c'or ne seroit mes ses amis
> avoec li tant con il soloit,
> quant il del vergier issir doit. †
> [6164–66]

She had depended for love upon a promise elicited in a dubious manner from her lover. Her authority must be challenged successfully before love, which requires free will, is possible.

For Enide (ll. 5786–828) the *Joie* is an unknown and ominous threat since she has been left behind. The fifty-line passage in which the couple part indicates that Chrétien conceived Erec's leave-taking as a significant moment: Enide will no longer physically be present to escort and influence her man.

Yet if Erec has regained his independence, it is not at the expense of love between the couple. In the middle of the parting scene, he reassures Enide explicitly:

> "De neant estes an esmai,
> car bien sachiez seüremant,
> s'an moi n'avoit de hardemant
> *fors tant con vostre amors m'an baille,*
> ne crienbroie je an bataille,
> cors a cors, nul home vivant." ‡
> [5804–9; my italics]

Enide's influence over Erec, no longer physical, is now purely moral or spiritual. This must be the sense of this

† that her lover would be no longer with her so much as he had been, inasmuch as he desired to leave the garden.

‡ "You are troubled without cause. But know this truly: if there were in me only so much courage as your love inspire, truly I should not fear to face any man alive."

last adventure and of the phrase *joie de la cort*. In true love there is no need to depend upon oaths (as in the case of Maboagrain and his lady[13]); and true love is not merely a physical relationship that excludes all else (as had been the case with Erec and Enide). Each state, constituting a sort of imprisonment, is inimical to the true nature of love. In freeing both himself and Maboagrain from their respective confinements, Erec has demonstrated to the world with a resounding horn call that *joie courtoise* is a transcending virtue.[14]

NOTES

1. Gaston Paris, in his review of Wendelin Foerster's edition of *Erec und Enide* (*Romania* 20 [1891]: 148–66), concludes that the *Joie de la Cort* constitutes a "récit absurde" and "incohérent" (p. 154).

2. Emmanuel Philippot, "Un Episode d'Erec et Enide: *La Joie de la cour*.—Mabon l'enchanteur," *Romania* 25 (1896): 258–94 ("*La Joie de la Cort* nous offre donc une version poétique de l'enserrement Merlin" [p. 283]; Helaine Newstead, "The *Joie de la Court* Episode in *Erec* and the Horn of Bran," *PMLA* 51 (1936): 13–25, cited p. 20; Roger S. Loomis, *Arthurian Tradition and Chrétien de Troyes* (New York: Columbia University Press, 1949), p. 170; William A. Nitze, "Erec and the Joy of the Court," *Speculum* 29 (1954): 691–701; Jean Frappier, *Chrétien de Troyes*, Connaissance des Lettres (Paris: Hatier, 1957), pp. 85–105.

3. Douglas Kelly, "La forme et le sens de la quête dans l'*Erec et Enide* de Chrétien de Troyes," *Romania* 92 (1971): 326–58. Kelly (p. 354) points out that the German version of *Erec* by Hartmann von Aue distorts Chrétien's concept of Enide. To the contrary, I believe that the German poet, in having Enide con-

demn Erec for his behavior following their marriage, may have been quite close to Chrétien's conception.

4. Used throughout this study is *Les Romans de Chrétien de Troyes*, vol. 1, *Erec et Enide*, ed. Mario Roques, Classiques Français du Moyen Age, no. 80 (Paris: H. Champion, 1952). The English translation is, with a few retouches of my own, that of W. Wistar Comfort, *Arthurian Romances by Chrétien de Troyes* (London: J. M. Dent, 1914).

5. Mario Roques, *Erec*'s editor, distinguishes between *joie* as a common noun and *Joie* when it refers properly to the adventure by using a capital letter. If my theory about the sense of the word *Joie* in this episode has any validity, it may be that several instances of *joie* (as in l. 5418) should be written as *Joie*.

6. Moshé Lazar, *Amour courtois et "fin' amors" dans la littérature du XIIe siècle*, Bibliothèque Française et Romane, series C, no. 8 (Paris: Klincksieck, 1964), pp. 77–78, equates, in the troubadours, *fals' amors* with *amors comunaus* and the latter, in Bernart de Ventadorn, with marriage based on mere "material interests."

7. I would propose *joie courtoise* as historically and ethically a more accurate name for what has since the time of Gaston Paris been designated with insufficient preciseness as *amour courtois*.

8. In the anonymous *Dame leale en amours*, edited by Arthur Piaget ("La *Belle Dame sans merci* et ses imitations," *Romania* 30 [1901]: 316–51), the poet wanders through a desolate valley strewn with "mains sarcus de corps trespassez" on his way to the court of the God of Love. In Achille Caulier, the *Cruelle Femme en amours*, edited by Piaget under the same title as above (*Romania* 31 [1902]: 315–49)—a response to the *Dame leale en amours*—the lovelorn poet laments in a desolate, noisome, dark valley.

9. See Howard Patch, *The Other World, According to Descriptions in Medieval Literature* (Cambridge: Harvard University Press, 1950) and Paul Piehler, *The Visionary Landscape* (London: Edward Arnold, 1971).

10. The early thirteenth-century *Le Fabel du Dieu d'Amours*, ed. Achille Jubinal (Paris: J. A. Merklein, 1834), makes use of

the same sort of Garden of Eden, exclusive preserve of the courtly world from which the *vilain* is excluded; it is explicitly the
domain of the King of Love. A gate and drawbridge are effective
barriers against those who are undesirable, but the way in which
these checks work automatically (pp. 15–16) is reminiscent of
Chrétien's wall of air.

11. Erec's quest is for the discovery of *amour courtois* for its
own sake and not in order to establish the primacy of chivalry
over love, or chivalry's dependence upon love as Douglas Kelly
believed.

12. William A. Nitze and Douglas Kelly have already shown
how Erec and Enide prove their love for one another in these
first adventures.

13. Zara P. Zaddy, *Chrétien Studies: Problems of Form and
Meaning in Erec, Yvain, Cligés, and the Charrete* (Glasgow: University of Glasgow Press, 1973), pp. 44, 56, holds that Maboagrain and his *amie* are merely a conventional courtly couple
who offer a bad example of ideal love: the lady completely
dominates her lover, and in this way "captures" him from the
rest of the feudal world. Maboagrain's oath of lifelong fidelity,
in which he promises to spar with all rivals who attempt to enter
his lady's garden, is undoubtedly a representation of the marriage vow. If one hesitates over the strange name of the luckless
knight, Maboagrain, it could be seen as an anagram for *bon
mariage*. In support of this reading one might consider the peculiar qualification that the knight himself makes about his name:
before coming to "cest païs" and while still a *vaslez* (i.e., before
being made a knight and being married), he had never used the
name Maboagrain, and had not even known it (ll. 6082–88). The
"hold" that the lady exercises over her lover has nothing mystical or enchanted about it: in granting her wish before he had understood its full implication—an understanding that came only
with his adulthood and his knighthood (ll. 6018–31)—he was
promising merely to enter the eternal state of holy matrimony.
By boldly approaching and sitting beside Maboagrain's lady in
the garden, Erec defied Maboagrain to do his worst, as a protec-

tive husband. When this worst does not turn out to be sufficient to maintain the lady's seclusion, the defeat, ignominious though it may be, frees Maboagrain from his lifetime obligation. For his part, Erec may also be unequivocally asserting his own independence from Enide. It would not, of course, be that Erec intends to exploit his freedom from Enide and turn into a profligate libertine by sitting beside every lady on every gold bed across all of the Celtic kingdoms: the act is just as symbolic with regard to his sensuous bond to Enide as it is symbolic of the dissolution of the absolute marriage vow with regard to Maboagrain and his lady. The two implications of the act are perhaps not too different: in both cases the married couples become freed to love their spouses freely and virtuously.

14. In his *Etudes sur le poème allégorique en France au moyen âge* (Bern: Editions Franke, 1971), Marc-René Jung, studying an interpretation of Psalm 44, *Eructavit cor meum*, notes the juxtaposition of a *joie de la cort* on the one hand and a *joie de paradis* or *joie esperités* on the other. The probable author of the interpretation, Adam de Perseigne, was writing at the court of Marie de Champagne around 1181–87.

Repetition and Variation
in Twelfth-Century French Romance

MATILDA TOMARYN BRUCKNER

In a postromantic society we no longer dismiss repetition out of hand as dead weight to be overcome in the pursuit of originality. Yet scholars and critics continue to apologize with phrases like "despite the repetition" or "not merely repetitive." Far from being opposed to originality, repetition and its familiar companions—imitation and convention—furnish the basic ingredients of medieval *inventio*. I would like to suggest how these principles contribute to medieval narrative. Repetition itself provides the main focus for this study, since imitations and conventions may be considered specific cases of the more general interplay between repetition and variation. The present work is based on an earlier analysis of hospitality as a conventional narrative sequence in French romance of the latter twelfth century.[1] The categories presented here to describe specific examples should be understood as the distillation of many close readings, not as formulas applied a priori to the romance texts.

How romancers invent and use their materials may be observed in a transitional moment where Yvain talks with one of his hosts:

> Mes sire Yvains tot escouta
> quan que ses ostes li conta,

> et quant trestot escouté ot,
> si li redist ce que lui plot.★
> [*Yvain*, vv. 3893–96]

At the literal level these verses serve as connectors, commonly found in romance and elsewhere to present speeches in direct and indirect discourse.[2] At the level of expression, repetition and variation enhance meaning: the act of listening is stated twice in alternation with the act of telling. Yvain listens to everything his host says, and when he has listened to everything, he responds with what pleases him. Metaphorically this transition offers a succinct description of how romances function both formally and thematically. A romancer listens to what is told in his own and others' romances. He listens well and, in response to the material heard, he "invents" his own narrative. Rhetorical treatises of the Middle Ages have a good deal to teach us about the process of *inventio*. Geoffroi de Vinsauf writes in his "Document on the Art of Versifying": "It is to be noted how difficult it is to treat well and appropriately common and familiar material. And how much more difficult, how much more praiseworthy it is to treat such material—that is, common and familiar—than other material—that is, new and unusual."[3] We are thus reminded that to invent in the medieval tradition is to discover—or rather to rediscover (cf. *trobar*, the Provençal term for writing or composing, which eventually leads to the Old French *trouver*:

★My lord Yvain listened to everything that his host told him, and when he had listened to everything, he in turn said to him what he pleased. [The translations given here are my own. They are as literal as possible, in order to catch the verbal play of repetition and variation that goes on within romance motifs.]

literary composition = finding). The romancer is part of a general audience, a consumer of literature, as well as one of the performers. The process of creating romance is renewed each time a listener follows and adapts the set of romance materials.

This exemplary description from *Yvain* raises two major issues to be explored here: first, the concept and operation of narrative blocks as a means to locate the interplay of repetition and variation; second, their function in the relationship between narrator and audience. While critics like Eugène Vinaver and William Ryding have focused primarily on overall structure,[4] I think it also useful to take a closer view of narrative composition as it develops along the syntagm, to concentrate on the "modular" quality of medieval narrative. Medieval romancers focus their primary attention not on single words, as Flaubert—or even Villon—might do, but on groups of narrative materials. The motif, or smallest narrative unit, is already a thematic constellation whose content can be realized in a variety of specific ways. While changes in verb tense, in descriptive details, or in syntactical patterns offer a range of possible variations, a nucleus of vocabulary carried over from one textual expression to another signals the presence of a given motif, to which I have given a name intended to summarize these possibilities. Motifs in romance thus function as "content-forms"[5]—that is, they tend to organize specific narrative inventions around a body of repeated actions (like "arming" and "greeting") or repeated descriptions (like *cortoisie* and food or drink). Such narrative blocks, even so small as motifs, orient the narrator's composition. Repetition and variation operate on each block; block joined to block forms the elaborate structures of romance.[6]

This is equally true if we consider the larger units of narrative that combine to map out a typical romance plot of the latter twelfth century. Peter Haidu, for example, taking two romances of Chrétien de Troyes as a basis for his model, describes the narrative structure of twelfth-century romance with the following schema: $A^1 + N^1 + X + A^2 + N^2$. An initial period of trial (which Haidu calls Approach one $= A^1$) is followed by success (Nexus one $= N^1$). When crisis intervenes (X), a second period of trial is necessitated (A^2), culminating in a second and final success for the hero (N^2). Both *Erec* and *Yvain* repeat this basic pattern. Variations occur when the narrator of *Floire* omits the preliminary approach to the first success, or when Gautier d'Arras doubles the entire structure to produce *Ille et Galeron*.[7]

In the corpus of romances that I have worked with, still other variations can be found. *Le Bel Inconnu* is particularly interesting in this respect, since it raises the possibility of knightly failure at the end of a romance. Its two love stories are not neatly resolved, as in *Ille*, but end on a suspended condition: if the narrator's lady is forthcoming, Guinglain will return to the good graces of his fairy love; if not, he will remain with his new wife (and second choice). The complexity of Guinglain's situation is reflected in the interlaced pattern of the two plot lines:

	quest	Fier Baiser	tourna-ment	Marriage
G. with B.E.	A^1	$+$ $N^1 + X$	$+$ $A^2 + N^2$	
G. with B.M.		$A^1 + N^1 +$	$X + A^2 + N^2 + X$	
		Ile d'Or	Mal Ile d'amour d'Or	

Viewed within the context of his love for Blances Mains, Guinglain's successful marriage with Blonde Esmeree (N^2) is a failure, not a satisfactory conclusion for the entire romance. The particular characteristics of *Le Bel Inconnu* may be defined by reference to the basic pattern and Renaut de Beaujeu's own variations: doubling, interlacing, and the extra unresolved crisis (X) that emphasizes its open-endedness.

This series of examples suggests how specific romances demonstrate their generic identity through repetition and their particular identity through variation. As with motifs, repetition and variation cannot be dissociated, since each provides the essential context for the other. Here then is my first reformulation: in medieval romance repetition and variation can be defined only in relation to each other. The critic may make generalizations that represent the common denominator in a group of texts, the literary tradition working in and between them. These abstractions constitute a guide for modern readers, especially necessary in medieval literature. The actual experience of the texts, however, shows that as soon as you have repetition, there is variation—and vice versa. It makes no sense to valorize variation at the expense of repetition: they are two sides of the same coin and equally valuable.

I have already suggested that narrative blocks locate the play of repetition and variation. In using Haidu's formula I may be working at a level too general to describe a narrative structure specific to romance. We might imagine other narratives that develop through similar stages. Yet if we focus on a more limited structure particular to twelfth-century French romance, we can see how the same techniques of repetition and variation still operate within typical narrative blocks. The romance motifs I mentioned earlier tend to form ordered sequences within juxtaposed adventures. These can readily be grouped by their thematic content: for example, sequences of combat or love matter frequently recur. I shall concentrate here on hospitality, a third staple of narrative sequence that often ties together the other two. In the French romances of the latter twelfth century, hospitality functions on a daily agenda; that is, narrators generally describe hospitality as an overnight sojourn, extending from vespers of one day till dawn of the next. The sequence of motifs that constitute hospitality form subunits: metonymic groupings within the syntagm, whose motifs are strongly associated, often implying each other when not specifically mentioned by the narrator. These subunits divide the hospitality narrative into four basic parts: I Welcome, II Suppertime, III Bedtime, IV Departure.

While this abstract four-part structure undergoes many transformations when manifested in particular romances, it does seem to operate, implicitly and explicitly, as a model of the romance tradition within which we can follow the variations of individual romancers. Some variations are frequent enough to be expressed in terms of the hospitality model itself. Narrators often elaborate upon the advance preparations that set the stage for hospitality. These form an additional subunit, I* Preliminary Arrangements, which takes its motifs primarily from the Welcome subunit and shifts them into the modalities of the future with promises, offers, or requests. It is also particularly open to motifs of identity and combat (and other less readily labeled materials), which make the transition to hospitality. Another important variation occurs when the narrator summarizes either completely or partially the daily agenda outlined above. If, for example, a guest requires special treatment over an extended period, Sojourn with Special Care (V) may substitute for Suppertime (II) and Bedtime (III). Motifs from II and III may appear, adjusted to the needs of a sick guest (as when wine is watered down for the wounded Erec). But V also supplies its own motifs: bathing, combing, sewing clothes, or even medical treatment may be in order. Like Preliminary Arrangements (I*), Sojourn with Special Care is more open to varied narrative materials, especially since the constraint of the daily agenda has been removed.

In turning now to some specific examples of hospitality, I am going to shift my focus from indirect relationships between romances, refracted through their common models, to direct contacts linking individual romances. Problems of chronology and imitation will thus enter into the discussion of repetition and variation. Consider a particular echo set up between *Yvain* (vv. 2884–3336) and *Partonopeu de Blois* (vv. 5975–6935): the rehabilitation initiated to bring the lover-gone-wild-man back to civilization. Chrétien's work precedes and is known by the anonymous author of *Partonopeu*.[8] In this case then *Yvain* must be the imitated and not the imitator. In both romances the wild-man convention is activated by an offense against love.[9] When a lady discovers the wild man, she identifies him after a lengthy process of investigation and invents a ruse that allows the knight to accept her offer of hospitality, which takes the form of an extended Sojourn with Special

Care and leads more or less directly to the knight's service in combat. The problem of unrealizable love (in addition to the knight's temporarily disturbed love) later arises in the context of hospitality and the exchange of courtly services—in *Yvain* through the actions and emotions of his hostess, the Lady of Noroison, and in *Partonopeu* through those of Persewis, Urraque's *suivante*.

This set of repetitions appears especially striking in the context of a subunit like Preliminary Arrangements, where the particulars of a given romance have a greater play in relation to the abstract model of hospitality. A comparison of subunit structures reinforces the echo between *Yvain* and *Partonopeu*. Repetition guides the opening and close of the sequences: I★ I V . . . IV.[10] Variation occurs in each sequence between V and IV: In *Yvain* a combat sequence intervenes, representing Yvain's service to his embattled hostess; in *Partonopeu* the hostess Urraque visits her sister Melior (IV★[ ]I) and so introduces a future combat sequence, the tournament in which Partonopeu will compete for Melior's hand in marriage.

The author of *Partonopeu* clearly shares Geoffroi's view about reusing familiar materials; he follows Chrétien's lead in constructing his own narrative throughout this episode and thus defines his romance, if only partially, in terms of Chrétien's (just as Chrétien defined *Cligès* partially in terms of *Tristan*). Such imitation goes beyond their shared membership in the romance genre, initiating a game of echo in which the second narrator must repeat a sufficient number of elements from the first to make his particular model evident to the reader/listener. While elsewhere narrators make explicit reference to their sources, here the allusion is implicit, calling for more alert participation from an audience of connoisseurs. But there is certainly no desire to conceal the process of repetition, since these particularly enhance the second narrator's skill.

Variation, always inseparable from repetition in romance practice, enters into the process of imitation. In this scene Partonopeu resembles Yvain, but he is also different: the familiar materials are reworked. Both hostesses use a ruse to offer hospitality properly, but the exact details correspond to different aspects of the same situation. The Lady of Noroison's *pucele* and her magic ointment return a sleeping Yvain to consciousness and sanity; the clothes she brings and leaves for him restore a certain respectability to the naked Yvain. He can then call for the young lady who happens to be passing by—her delicacy is magnificently demonstrated in this last detail of her ruse—and request hospitality (already well underway) in exchange for his offer of service in combat (equally anticipated by the *pucele*). The change from an unconscious to a conscious victim requires a different strategy from Urraque. Partonopeu is willfully refusing life because of his betrayal of Melior. Urraque's ruse is not quite magic but very much like it: the power of fiction, a "fause noveile" that will permit the exchange to take place but will also require it to remain secret. Urraque pretends that Melior has forgiven Partonopeu and sent her to care for him. The very love problem that earlier in their conversation prevented Partonopeu from accepting hospitality is thus resolved (at least in Partonopeu's mind) and now requires him to accept Urraque's service.

Those familiar with the two romances will recognize

that *Partonopeu*'s imitation of *Yvain* continues outside this particular episode, for example in Lunete's role as mediator between knight and lady, her secret hospitality vouchsafed for Yvain in the midst of Laudine's hostility. Imitation in medieval romance has traditionally been treated under the category of source studies, which tend to assign greater value to the "original." Recent critics have begun to use the notion of *intertextualité*, a suggestive term (and certainly more neutral to our modern ears).[11] Its appearance signals more complex and varied points of view now available for analyzing contacts between literary works. Yet modern theorists of intertextuality have thus far tended to neglect the specificity of medieval literature, the voluntary and open character of its exchanges. Here we need something more specific to medieval narrative composition. In that context, imitation is best understood as a special subheading of repetition and variation, as described above. Again, value cannot be situated on one side of the relationship and excluded from the other, since both are mutually reinforcing. Chrétien is here imitated by the author of *Partonopeu*; elsewhere he imitates (whether his model be *Tristan*, *Eneas*, or himself). A poetic of (intertextual) references operates throughout twelfth-century French romance; imitation calls attention to the network of cross-references linking romances to each other and to the entire literary tradition. No romance of this period exists by itself as a closed text, though we may read them so with some success. Romances respond specifically to each other and generally to the romance tradition. This dynamic may be seen expanding in the thirteenth century as continuations multiply and the immense cycles of Lancelot and the

Grail stories are assembled. But it is already operating in the romances of the twelfth century. Even where allusions are not made explicit, they are neither denied (this would on the contrary signal an allusion) nor deviously hidden.

Medieval tradition does not mask repetition; it plays on it. Narrators comment directly and indirectly on what they are doing, how, and why. A dialogue between the narrator and his public accompanies and informs his orderly disposition of narrative materials, the articulations of which are made explicit in a number of ways: through "personal" interventions, humorous and ironic overtones, certain uses of summary (see below), and self-reflexive commentary in which the text looks at itself, naming what has just been or is about to be told—as in the rhetorical device of *transitio*. These articulations are useful both structurally and aesthetically.

We are moving now into the second major issue mentioned earlier: the role that narrative blocks play in the dialogue between narrator and audience. In the oral context of medieval romance, read aloud to a courtly public, as we see for example in *Yvain* (vv. 5356–64), it is not surprising that narrative elaboration focuses on familiar blocks, inviting the audience to perceive repetition and variation within the recognizable. These narrative blocks might be compared to the *loci* ("backgrounds" or "common places") recommended in the *Rhetorica Ad Herennium* for the exercise of the artificial memory.[12] A set of places is to be memorized in a given order—a series of rooms perhaps, through which the memory can tour backward and forward. Such places can then function as ordered units in the memory, reusable with the specific content of any giv-

en speech. *Ad Herennium*'s importance for the Middle Ages
has been discussed by Ernst Robert Curtius and Edmond
Faral.[13] Though recognition and memorization are not
identical procedures, I have introduced this comparison
because it suggests an awareness of repetition as a thought
process, recalling twelfth-century French romance.

With the concept of narrative block, we can pass back
and forth between authorial invention and audience perception, and consequently move on to the third term I
intend to reevaluate: convention. As with imitation, it operates as a special subheading of repetition and variation.
A convention is a set of repetitions and variations that
typically appear together, recognizable as such by the
romance public.[14] Variations are as much a part of the convention as repetition. Recurrent elements (like the four-
part structure described above) signal the existence of a
convention like hospitality, for example, but the full actu-
alization of hospitality sequences depends on the play between repetition and variation. New or different details
can be integrated within the typical framework of hospitality, without endangering its status as convention. When
Floire spills his wine, for instance (*Floire et Blancheflor*, vv.
1115–17), he does what no other guest of twelfth-century
romance does, yet his action is clearly contained within the
typical subunit, Suppertime. The "unconventional" describes elements not usually part of the tradition received
or, alternatively, elements of that tradition used in an unexpected context, creating new meaning or generating unusual associations. These stretch the domain of romance to
what lies beyond the already said. The "anticonventional"

turns conventions upside down, exploring the capacity of romance to absorb its opposite (cf. the "antihospitality" of the hermit in *Yvain*, who runs inside his house and hopes his "guest" will never return, vv. 2834–60). Together the conventional, the unconventional, and the anticonventional gain meaning from their mutual reflections. As with repetition and variation, there is not convention in one corner, nonconvention in another, but a continual give-and-take between them at all levels of the narrative.

I would like to present a last set of examples to demonstrate how these general statements on convention apply to specific texts. I have already discussed some direct and indirect contacts between romances, but as yet I have not analyzed how romancers repeat themselves within the confines of a single romance. Inevitably, even such a concentration on one romance will lead us back to the romance tradition. The opening of *Yvain* provides a well-known example of hospitality, when Calogrenant sleeps at a *vavasseur*'s before and after the adventure at the magic fountain. There are in fact three sequences of hospitality narrated in alternation with the intervening combat sequence and Yvain's departure from Arthur's court (*Yvain*, vv. 198–275, 554–76, 777–92). I have chosen this example because it presents a high degree of recognizability and self-consciousness on the part of the narrators (Chrétien and Calogrenant[15]). Calogrenant's first overnight sojourn is recounted in great detail: it moves through all the basic units of the hospitality sequence (I–IV). Both host and guest demonstrate in conversation what they know about the customs surrounding hospitality, the host when he

laments how long it has been since he last lodged a knight
errant, Calogrenant when he accepts the *preudome*'s request
that the reward for hospitable service be a second opportunity to present it (vv. 254–66). The model of hospitality
is explicitly established in the narrative, as well as the occasion for repetition and variation when Calogrenant returns
to his host.

The following sequences create a descending pattern at
the narrative level, as Chrétien uses summaries more and
more to replace the basic subunits (sequence 2: I* I résumé;
sequence 3: résumé). Concurrently, an ascending pattern
builds up at the content level, as each succeeding sequence
is based on a comparison with the first experience of hospitality. The second sequence, Calogrenant's return, is
equal in hospitality to the first night. But by the time
Yvain arrives at the *vavasseur*'s, expectations have risen so
much—in him and in the audience—from Calogrenant's
and the narrator's tales that the hospitality now described
(sequence 3) is superior to that of the first visit. Hyperbole
helps create the rise in expectations:

> La nuit ot, ce poez savoir,
> tel oste com il vost avoir;
> car plus de bien et plus d'enor
> trueve il assez el vavasor
> que ne vos ai conté et dit;
> et an la pucele revit
> de san et de biauté cent tanz
> que n'ot conté Calogrenanz,
> qu'an ne puet pas dire la some
> de prode fame et de prodome,
> des qu'il s'atorne, a grant bonté.

Ja n'iert tot dit ne tot conté
que leingue ne puet pas retreire
tant d'enor con prodon fet feire.†
[vv. 777–90]

Chrétien's ironic play, especially his skillful use of summary to replace and allude to all the detailed services of
hospitality already described elsewhere, has considerably
increased since the more serious and straightforward ex-
ploitation of hospitality in *Erec*. Clearly such narrative
games are possible only within a conventional structure
where we know what has been left out. The delicate balance between surprise and expectation is achieved by repeating and changing a recognizable pattern—recognized
by the narrator and the participants within the text, by the
romance public outside the text.

Narrators also play on our expectation of where hospitality sequences should occur in the narrative. A combination of motifs typically signals the opening for a hospitality
sequence: the knight rides along his route; vespers nears;
a lodging is sighted.

Chevalchié ont, des le matin
jusqu'al vespre, le droit chemin,
plus de .xxx. liues galesches,

---

† That night he had, you can be sure, a host such as he desired; for he
found in the vavasor more goodness and more honor than I've told you
and spoken of; and in the maiden he saw one hundred times more sense
and beauty than Calogrenant had spoken of, for one couldn't tell the
sum of a lady or a good man's qualities, once he gives himself to goodness. It couldn't all be told or counted since the tongue can't speak about
as much honor as a good man can do.

> tant qu'il sont devant les bretesches
> d'un chastel fort et riche et bel.‡
>
> [*Erec*, vv. 5319–23]

Time and place are right: hospitality is no doubt soon to begin. In *Le Bel Inconnu*, as Guinglain rides with Helie on the way to *Gaste Cité*, Renaut de Beaujeu plays on this recognition and expectation in three successive hospitality sequences (at Bucleus, Ile d'Or, and Galigan).[16] Each time the typical motifs signal an opening for the hospitality sequence; each time hospitality is deferred and our expectation frustrated by the intervention of a combat sequence. Once the combat is completed, hospitality unfolds with no further surprises: our expectation is belatedly fulfilled. By the time Guinglain arrives at Lanpar's, the third stop in the series, the reader/listener has been conditioned to expect precisely the unexpected. In fact, Renaut capitalizes on this new expectation by making the custom of Galigan require combat as the price for hospitality: what was unconventional at Bucleus has become a new convention at Lanpar's.

The problem of value judgments remains open here: are certain imitations good or bad, successful or unsuccessful? This question should not, however, prevent us from seeing that only the conventionality of hospitality (or of any other traditional materials) allows romancers to play as they do with narrative and audience. Without the game of recognition, modulated through repetitions and variations, the most remarkable feats of a Chrétien or a Renaut

‡They rode from morning till vespers, the right road, more than thirty Welsh leagues, till they came before the towers of a castle strong and rich and beautiful.

de Beaujeu would be impossible. Yet the critical attitude toward repetition is still largely negative. My intention here is to prevent modern judgments of repetition, imitation, and convention from blocking our appreciation of how they were used in medieval literature. What makes Chrétien's romances stand out with special brilliance from those of his contemporaries is precisely his skillful manipulation of the common and familiar. Through repetition —and invention—his works become "more difficult and praiseworthy," providing a rich resource for those who follow.[17]

NOTES

1. See my "Hospitality: A Narrative Model in Twelfth-Century French Romances (1160 to 1200)," *DAI* 36 (1975): 267A. In order to survey the possibilities open to twelfth-century romancers, I chose a corpus of eight romances, four Arthurian—Chrétien de Troyes, *Erec et Enide* (CFMA, 80) and *Le Chevalier au lion* (*Yvain*) (CFMA, 89), ed. M. Roques (Paris: Champion, 1955 and 1960 respectively); Gautier d'Arras, *Ille et Galeron*, ed. F. Cowper (Paris: Picard, 1956); Renaut de Beaujeu, *Le Bel Inconnu*, ed. G. Perrie Williams (Paris: Champion, 1967)—and four non-Arthurian—Aimon de Varennes, *Florimont: Ein Altfranzösischer Abenteuerroman*, ed. A. Hilka (Göttingen: Max Niemeyer, 1932); *Floire et Blancheflor*, ed. M. Pelan (Paris: Publications de la Faculté des Lettres de l'Université de Strasbourg, 1956); Hue de Rotelande, *Ipomedon*, ed. E. Kölbing and E. Koschwitz (Breslau: Wilhelm Koebner, 1889); *Partonopeu de Blois*, ed. J. Gildea, O.S.A. (Villanova, Pa.: Villanova University Press, 1967).

2. Cf. the speech formulas discussed by Joseph Duggan in his work on *chansons de geste*: "Formulas in the *Couronnement de*

Louis," *Romania* 87 (1966): 315–44; *The "Song of Roland": Formulaic Style and Poetic Craft* (Berkeley: University of California Press, 1973), pp. 115–16.

3. *Documentum de Arte Versificandi*, pt. 2, sect. 3, p. 132, cited in Edmond Faral, *Les Arts poétiques du XIIe et du XIIIe siècles: Recherches et documents sur la technique littéraire du Moyen Age* (1924; rpt. Paris: Champion, 1971), p. 309: "Post praedicta est notandum quod difficile est materiam communem et usitatem convenienter et bene tractare. Et quanto difficilius, tanto laudabilius est bene tractare materiam talem, scilicet communem et usitatem, quam materiam aliam, scilicet novam et inusitatem."

4. See, for example, Eugène Vinaver's *Rise of Romance* (New York: Oxford University Press, 1971) or William Ryding's *Structure in Medieval Narrative* (The Hague: Mouton, 1971).

5. Louis Hjelmslev, *Prolégomènes à une théorie du langage* (Paris: Minuit, 1968), p. 52.

6. Cf. Robert Jordan in his introduction to *Chaucer and the Shape of Creation* (Cambridge: Harvard University Press, 1967), pp. 3–54. He compares narrative structure to the architecture of a Gothic cathedral: "Construction is an additive process which consists in the patterned disposition of finite elements, namely the basic module, repetitions of it, and multiples of it" (p. 53).

7. "Narrative Structure in *Floire et Blancheflor*: A comparison with Two Romances of Chrétien de Troyes," *Romance Notes* 14 (1972): 383–86:

$$(- \; +) \; N^1 + X + A^2 + N^2.$$

"Narrativity and Language in Some Twelfth Century Romances," *Yale French Studies* 51 (1974): 133–46:

Ille w/ Galeron	$A^1 + N^1 + X + A^2 + N^2 + X$
Ille w/ Ganor	$A^1 + N^1 + X \;\; + A^2 + N^2.$

8. See A. Fourrier, *Le Courant réaliste en France au moyen âge, I: Les débuts (XIIe siècle)* (Paris: Nizet, 1960), p. 391. *Yvain* was written about 1177; *Partonopeu* between 1182 and 1185, according to Fourrier.

9. In *Wild Men in the Middle Ages: A Study in Art, Sentiment, and Demonology* (Cambridge: Harvard University Press, 1952), pp. 27–29, Richard Bernheimer gives some attention to the *vilain* whom Calogrenant and Yvain meet on their way to the fountain. But he mentions only in passing how Yvain, like Lancelot and Tristan, falls into temporary madness and lives the forest life of a wild man (p. 14). Many literary aspects of the convention remain to be explored (for example, the parallel between Yvain and the *vilain* within Chrétien's romance, the romance hero as temporary wild man, the role of love—courtly or otherwise—as a motivation for wild-man transformations, and others).

10. A departure does close both sequences, but Partonopeu's is not exactly identical to Yvain's. Partonopeu and his hostess leave together to visit Melior, then return again to stay in Salence until the tournament (at which point Partonopeu accidentally leaves because of a change in wind while boating). The whole series may be divided into three related sequences (a. vv. 5979–6436, 6799–935; b. vv. 6936–44, 7407–30, 7581–84, 7605–8; c. 7627–50), with the middle one particularly irregular in terms of the hospitality model.

11. See, for example, Julia Kristeva, *Le Texte du roman: approche sémiologique d'une structure discursive transformationelle* (The Hague: Mouton, 1970), pp. 12, 14, 67–69, 139–76; *Semeiotikè: recherches pour une sémanalyse* (Paris: Seuil, 1969), pp. 146, 255–57; Michael Riffaterre, "Describing Poetic Structures: Two Approaches to Baudelaire's *Les Chats*" in *Structuralism*, ed. J. Ehrmann (1966; rpt. New York: Anchor Books, 1970), pp. 188–230 (cf. his notion of the "superreader," pp. 202–4).

12. [Cicero], trans. Harry Caplan (Cambridge, Mass.: Loeb Classics, 1964), pp. 208–25, XV.27–XXIV.40 (especially XVII.30). For a detailed discussion of the artificial memory, see Frances Yates's *The Art of Memory* (Chicago: University of Chicago Press, 1966), p. 21. The first three chapters treat classical and medieval arts of memory.

13. Ernst Robert Curtius, *European Literature and the Latin*

Middle Ages, trans., Willard R. Trask (New York: Harper and Row, 1963), pp. 65–66; Edmond Faral, pp. 48–54.

14. Cf. Paul Zumthor's work on the "registre" of the *chant courtois* in *Langues et techniques poétiques à l'époque romane, XIe–XIIIe siècles* (Paris: Klincksieck, 1963), pp. 141–52. When he deals with romance in his *Essai de poétique médiéval* (Paris: Seuil, 1972), pp. 339–80, he seems to emphasize especially the openness of romance in comparison with the closed system of the lyric "registre." Perhaps it is just a question of degree, but I do think it is important to remember how highly formalized romance, especially twelfth-century romance, remains: romance is a "system" open to a greater variety of materials, but these are still firmly held within the organization of romance conventions (as Zumthor himself demonstrates in his analyses).

15. The increase in self-consciousness is confirmed by Chrétien's extensive use of Calogrenant's first person. Though many sequences of hospitality are reported in direct discourse in my corpus of romances, Calogrenant's narrative is the only one that develops beyond a short summary and the only one that describes a sequence of hospitality not otherwise presented by the narrator.

16. *Le Bel Inconnu*, vv. 1497–869, 1870–2474, 2491–841.

17. I would like to express my gratitude to Nancy Regalado and Evelyn Birge Vitz for their generous encouragement and criticism essential to the process of refining my ideas and to their presentation in this paper.

IV

Expansion and
Transformations

Narrative Transformations
of Twelfth-Century Troubadour Lyric

LOWANNE E. JONES

ithin the first half of the thirteenth century there appeared in the Old Occitan language three new narrative forms that are directly related to the love lyric tradition of the preceding century. The first of these is the short story or *novas*, a straightforward narrative composed in octosyllabic couplets ranging from several hundred to several thousand verses. The second is the largely allegorical narrative, which is another development of the *novas* or *romans*.[1] The third consists of the short prose troubadour biographies known as *vidas* and the fourteenth-century prose explanations or *razos* used to introduce troubadour poems. As far as we know, these four forms, *novas*, allegorical narrative, *vidas*, and *razos*, did not exist in Occitan before 1220.

The earliest extant *novas* is "Abril issi'e mays intrava," a 1,773-verse *ensenhamen* composed by the Catalan troubadour Raimon Vidal de Besalú between 1196 and 1213.[2] Of the three surviving narrative allegories, the earliest is probably the *Cort d'Amor*.[3] It is a poem of 1,721 lines written by an anonymous near-contemporary of the Gascon troubadour Guiraut de Calanso, whose own poem "A lieis cui am," probably written before 1204, is the first preserved lyric allegory in Old Occitan.[4] The earliest *vidas*, attributed to Uc de Saint-Circ, date from approximately the first third of the thirteenth century.[5]

Each of these early thirteenth-century examples is closely linked to the lyric tradition of the twelfth century. The subject matter of these new genres is that of the lyrics, generally with considerable elaboration and development. Quotations of famous lines from the lyrics are frequent and are often accompanied by discussions of their meaning or import. Finally, the authors of these early narratives apparently seek to preserve the heritage of the classical Occitan love lyric by recalling the courtly atmosphere of the Golden Age of the Occitan lyric tradition. These transformations of lyric elements into narrative forms were prompted, at least in part, by changes in the attitudes of both poets and audiences.

Some of the narrative roots of the thirteenth-century *novas* can be traced to the short narrative forms of the twelfth century, especially the *ensenhamens*, poems addressed to a jongleur in order to describe and prescribe his poetic repertoire. The earliest extant example is "Cabra juglar,"[6] a poem of 146 lines written by Guiraut de Cabreira in about 1160 and listing epics and romances, ancient as well as medieval, knowledge of which was indispensable to any successful jongleur. By the thirteenth century the scope of the *ensenhamen* had expanded, and Guiraut de Calanso reminds his jongleur that it would be wise to know a good deal about the personification of love and its allegorical nature.[7] The didactic quality of the *ensenhamen*, together with the fact that Guiraut felt the need to instruct both the jongleur and his audience in the nature and attributes of love, indicates a new development in the concerns of both troubadour and audience.

Guiraut de Cabreira's jongleur apparently needed to know only the tales then circulating. Guiraut de Calanso's jongleur, on the other hand, needed a working definition of *fin' amor*, as though he could no longer be certain of an informed or sympathetic audience. It is possible that Guiraut de Calanso was stressing only the importance of his own compositions, saying in effect: "You must know the song I wrote about the goddess Love," but whatever the case, the thirteenth-century jongleur apparently had to be reminded that either the troubadour who hired him or the audience that heard him required the allegory of love to be clear. Guiraut de Calanso's advice reflects the altered perceptions of the early thirteenth-century poets, and also, presumably, the interests or possibly even the ignorance of their audiences.

Raimon Vidal's long *ensenhamen* "Abril issia" represents an early form of the *novas*, combining both *ensenhamen* and vaguely autobiographical elements typical of the *vidas*. Early in "Abril issia," a young jongleur laments the decline of poetry, hospitality, and the courtly tradition. In response an older troubadour nostalgically recalls days gone by, remembering men and women of merit, hoping to instill in the young performer an appreciation of courtly life as it once was. He continues with advice and examples, including inspiring quotations from the lyrics of Guiraut de Bornelh, Arnaut de Marueil, Bertran de Born, Raimon de Miraval, and Peire Rogier. Evidently hoping to foster in his companion a zeal for reviving and maintaining the courtly life, the poet also appreciates the young man's craft and offers sound and practical observations related to professional performance.

In this *novas* Raimon's tendency to quote lines from the poems of other troubadours lends authoritative support to the arguments put forth, preserves and even enshrines famous verses, and recreates the nobility of the past while suggesting the poverty and decadence of the present. The pedantic tone is consistent with the didactic aims of the poem.

Similarly, in Raimon's second *novas*, "So fo e·l temps c'om era iays,"[8] (commonly known as the *Judici d'Amor*), Sir Uc de Mataplana quotes other troubadours: Raimbaut de Vaqueiras, Bertran de Born, Peire Vidal, Folquet de Marselha, Uc Brunet, Gaucelm Faidit, Bernart de Ventadorn, Raimon de Miraval, and an anonymous poet. It is interesting to note that the subject of this *novas* recalls the principal episode of certain *tensos* and *partimens* of the twelfth century: the rejection of a knight by a lady and his subsequent submission to a second lady, whereupon an authority is requested to determine which lady has rightful claim to the knight's service. Ordinarily a *tenso* or *partimen* that debated this question would end with the matter unresolved, the opinion of another authority being sought in the *envoi*. Raimon's *Judici d'Amor* simply extends the lyric format to include the final judgment. Once again the subject, tone, and citations are grounded in the twelfth-century lyric.

Raimon's last extant narrative, "Unas novas vos vuelh comtar,"[9] known by the title *Castia-Gilos* given it by Alfonso VIII of Castile, no longer exhibits the transitional characteristics that relate the two earlier *novas* to the lyric tradition. Rather it recounts in 450 lines the theme of the jealous husband so precisely elaborated later in the *novas del Papagai* and in the romance of *Flamenca*.[10] *Castia-Gilos* contains no laments for the courtly days of old, no citations from the troubadours, and no references to them. Instead it may be aligned with the French fabliau tradition of tales relating with relish the duping of the cuckold.

The earliest allegorical *novas*, the unfinished *Cort d'Amor*, represents a further development within this tradition: self-sufficient allegory. In this instance the anonymous poet addressed himself not to a jongleur but to a group of twenty-eight *donas* and *pulsellas*. An introductory lecture on the nature of love is pronounced by *Fin'Amor* to her twelve allegorical barons. However, the ladies in the audience require further elaboration on the specifics of love, in the form of an *ensenhamen* by Cortezia. Numerous lectures and sermons on various aspects of love follow, all addressed to the court at large, with the exception of a lecture given by the Bailiff of Love, who tailors her description of the *jazer* specifically for the maidens in the audience.

Like Raimon Vidal's early *novas*, the *Cort d'Amor* lies squarely in the lyric tradition, where personification, including that of *Fin' Amor*, is fundamental.[11] Of the twelve barons of *Fin' Amor* in the *Cort d'Amor*, eight can be traced to earlier *cansos*. *Joi, Cortezia, Pretz, Largueza*, and *Drudaria* are often personified by Marcabru. *Solatz* appears in "A gran honor viu cui jois es cobitz" (l. 2) by Arnaut de Marueil, *Bon'Esperansa* (as *Bon'Esper*) in "En un sonet gai e leugier" (ll. 5–10) by Daude de Pradas, and *Domneis* in

Peire d'Alvernha's "Deiosta·ls breus jorns" (l. 48). *Dousa Compania*, *Ardiment*, *Paors*, and *Celamens* so far have been impossible to locate as personifications although they abound as lexical items in the *cansos*. Of the *Cort d'Amors'* seven peers and seven enemies of love, all but the *Bailessa d'Amor* and *Malparliers* are found in the *cansos*. Of the enemies, *Orguelh*, *Malvestat*, and *Cobezesa* are used repeatedly by Marcabru. *Putaria* can be traced to *Putia* in his "Per l'aura freida que guida" (l. 26), and perhaps *Fals Semblantz* to *Falsedatz* in "Lo vers comenssa" (l. 42). *Vilania* is introduced by Peirol in "Camjat ai mon consirer" (l. 36). Among the peers of love, *Honor*, *Valor*, *Jovens*, and *Proeza* appear frequently in Marcabru. *Merce* is personified by Arnaut de Marueil in "Aissi cum selh que tem qu'Amors l'aucia" (ll. 18, 20) and other poems. *Sens* may perhaps be related to personifications of Razos. Thus, the allegorical characters of the *Cort d'Amor* are neither descendants of Latin mythology nor visitors from France.

Both the *Cort d'Amor* and Raimon Vidal's "Abril issia" are didactic works intended for the edification of a younger generation. Whereas Raimon leans on the authority of the earlier troubadours he names, the author of the *Cort d'Amor* simply borrows verses and images from them, apparently assuming, probably correctly, that the sources would be recognized. Certainly the longer, more obvious references like the parable of the thief, borrowed from Perdigon, and the fable of the stag, borrowed from Guillem de Montanhagol, were easily recognized.[12] It is quite possible that much of the pleasure taken in this poem lay precisely in this identification of themes and motifs bor-

rowed from popular song. Whatever the case, it is clear
that the author of the *Cort d'Amor* intended such quotations to carry moral weight and authority, much as biblical
quotations would in moral tracts and popular literature.

Like Raimon Vidal, the author of the *Cort d'Amor* assumes a youthful and ignorant audience. In part this assumption is inherent in the subject of the sermons: one
does not ordinarily lecture the aged or the experienced on
the subject of love, while the ignorance of innocent maidens in such matters is assumed. But it seems to be another
sign of the times that the precepts under discussion require
such extensive elucidation. Not only the fine points (as in
many of the *tensos* or *partimens* of the twelfth century) but
also the very concept of fine love here require clarification
—a situation inconceivable in the Golden Age.

Occitan allegories from the middle or end of the thirteenth century gradually yield to Latin and French influences. A case in point is "Lai on cobra sos dregz estats,"[13]
in which Love, the female personification of twelfth-century Occitan lyrics, is accompanied by the male god of
love who appears in Ovid and Andreas Capellanus.

The very existence of the *vidas* and *razos* illustrates the
changes after the twelfth century. It is a common assumption that these short prose narratives were as a rule composed not by troubadours but by jongleurs who felt a need
in performance for explanatory materials. The creation of
the *vidas* and *razos* apparently was dictated by the audience's faulty memory for biographical information and its
inability to comprehend fully the context, the characters,
or the images of the poems. The composition of the *vidas*

and *razos* by a jongleur, who was often less skilled and less scrupulous than the troubadour whose songs he sang, explains that the *vidas* contain honest mistakes as well as blatantly fabricated information. Often a *razo* bears little relation to the lyric it purports to clarify. A later hybrid form combined biography with commentary to produce substantial narratives of considerable fantasy which came to resemble the *novas*.[14]

Like Raimon Vidal and the *Cort d'Amor*, the authors of the *vidas* and *razos* maintain the viability of the twelfth-century *canso d'amor*. It was, after all, their stock in trade; they could ill afford to allow several thousand lyrics and melodies to go out of style. Even more important to the jongleurs was the preservation of the Occitan courts and the entire courtly mode of life which supported their art. Small wonder then that the jongleurs framed the twelfth-century love lyrics in a narrative context of their own invention designed to recall and clarify the Golden Age that had produced them.

Each of these new genres—*novas*, allegory, *vida*, and *razos*—was directly inspired by the troubadour lyrics of the preceding generations. The earliest examples of these new forms reproduce subject, tone, and actual verses from twelfth-century *cansos*. Each narrative type is a response to the evolving tastes of the thirteenth century which threatened—through economic and geographical dislocation, changing fashions, ignorance, and apathy—to extinguish the love lyric tradition. It is ironic that these new forms, by virtue of their own popularity, were to further the decline of the *canso d'amor*.

NOTES

The research for this article was supported by the Ohio State University Graduate School University Small Research Grants Program no. 7404.

1. These two terms are used interchangeably in the thirteenth-century tradition, with *novas* designating shorter versions, *romans* generally referring to longer ones. I would make a distinction here between more-or-less "original" allegorical compositions and translations of allegories. The Occitan *Boecis*, an early translation of Boethius's *Consolation of Philosophy*, is not, then, a part of this tradition.

2. Preserved in MS β^2; see Alfred Pillet and Henry Carstens, *Bibliographie der Troubadours* (Halle/Saale, 1933 rpt. New York: Burt Franklin, 1968), p. xxxi. Ed.: "Abrils issi'e mays intrava," ed. Wilhelm Bohs, *Romanische Forschungen* 15 (1904): 216–96; extracts with Spanish translation in Manuel Milá y Fontanals, *De los trovadores en España*, 2d ed. (Barcelona: A. Verdaguer, 1889), pp. 295–312; and *Raimon Vidal, Poetry and Prose*, vol. 2, "Abril issia," ed. W. H. Field, Studies in the Romance Languages and Literatures, no. 110 (Chapel Hill: University of North Carolina Press, 1971). The text contains a reference (ll. 737–38 in Field) to Peire II of Aragon, who reigned 1196–1213, as a living king.

3. Preserved in a single manuscript: MS. N, currently MS. M 819 in the Pierpont Morgan Library. See *The "Cort d'Amor": A Thirteenth-Century Allegorical Art of Love*, ed. Lowanne E. Jones, Studies in the Romance Languages and Literatures, no. 185 (Chapel Hill: University of North Carolina Press, 1977).

4. Otto Dammann, *Die allegorische Canzone des Guiraut de Calanso "A lieis cui am de cor e de saber" und ihre Deutung*, (Breslau: W. Koeber, 1891), pp. 11–29. This edition was reprinted with French translation in *Les Troubadours*, René Nelli and René Lavaud, eds. (Bruges: Desclée de Brouwer, 1966), 2: 651–53.

H. R. Jauss, "Entstehung and Strukturwandel der allegorischen Dichtung," pt. 5, "Die Minneallegorie als esoteriche Form einer neuen *ars amandi*," *Grundriss der romanischen Literaturen des Mittelalters*, vol. 6, pt. 1 (Heidelberg: Carl Winter, 1968), p. 230, dates this poem between 1196 and 1202.

5. *Les Biographies des troubadours, Textes provençaux des XIIIe et XIVe siècles*, eds. Jean Boutière and A.-H. Schutz, 2d ed. (Paris: Nizet, 1964), pp. vii–x.

6. Karl Bartsch, *Denkmäler der provenzalischen Litteratur*, Bibliothek des Litterarischen Vereins, no. 39 (Stuttgart, 1856), pp. 88–94.

7. "Fadet joglar," ibid., pp. 94–101.

8. Preserved in two manuscripts. Ed.: C. A. F. Mahn, *Gedichte der Troubadours* (Berlin: F. Duemmler, 1862), 2: 23–27; portions reprinted by Milá y Fontanals, pp. 289–93; and Nelli-Lavaud, 2: 170–85.

9. Preserved in MS. N. Eds.: F.-J.-M. Raynouard, *Choix des poésies originales des troubadours* (Paris: F. Didot, 1816), 3: 420–30; Carl Appel, *Provenzalische Chrestomathie*, 6th ed. (Leipzig: Reisland, 1930), pp. 193–97; Irénée Cluzel, *L'Ecole des Jaloux (Castiagilos): Fabliau du XIIIe siècle par le troubadour catalan Raimon Vidal de Bezalú* (Paris: Les amis de la langue d'oc, 1958), reprinted in Nelli-Lavaud, 2: 186–211.

10. For editions of the *Novas del Papagai*, Raynouard, *Choix*, 2: 275–82; K. Bartsch, *Chrestomathie provençale*, 6th ed. (Marburg, 1904), cols. 283–92, reprinted in Nelli-Lavaud, 2: 218–35. For *Flamenca*, see *The Romance of Flamenca, a Provençal Poem of the Thirteenth Century*, ed. Marion E. Porter, trans. Merton J. Hubert (Princeton: Princeton University Press, 1962); and other editions.

11. Some troubadours tend particularly toward personification and allegory: Arnaut de Marueil (19 different personifications in 21 of his 25 lyric poems); Daude de Pradas (13 in 10 of his 17 lyric poems); Peire Cardenal (17 personifications in the first stanza of "Falsedatz e Desmezura" alone); and Marcabru (28 in all).

12. Cf. *Les Chansons de Perdigon*, ed. Henry J. Chaytor, CFMA 53 (Paris: Champion, 1926), "Tot l'an mi ten amors d'aital faisso," ll. 10–18; and *Les Poésies de Guilhem de Montanhagol, troubadour provençal du XIIIe siècle*, ed. Peter J. Ricketts (Toronto: Pontifical Institute of Mediaeval Studies, 1964), "Non estarai, per ome qu·m casti," ll. 27–45.

13. K. Bartsch, *Chrestomathie*, cols. 291–96.

14. Examples of such fabrications, errors, and fantasies are easily found: the *vida* of Jaufre Rudel describes a love affair with the Countess of Tripoli, largely derived from his poetry (Boutière, pp. 16–17); the *razos* to Peire Vidal's poetry tend to take the form of short stories, of which several are based on the stolen-kiss theme and one is devoted to the beating he received disguised as a wolf for love of La Loba of Pennautier (Boutière, pp. 356–74); the *vida* of Guilhem de Cabestaing, with the eaten heart motif (Boutière, pp. 530–36), is an excellent paradigm of the hybrid form.

Transformations of Courtly Love Poetry

Vita Nuova and *Canzoniere*

SARA STURM-MADDOX

rom one point of view, to combine Dante's *Vita Nuova* and Petrarch's *Canzoniere* in a discussion of the transformations of courtly love poetry may suggest a routine critical exercise. The centrality of the courtly lyric tradition in both works is immediately apparent in their amatory content and, more specifically, in the poetic expression of that content in individual poems. From another perspective, however, their combination may appear problematic: while Dante's early work is often considered in relation to the earlier lyric tradition, invoked overtly in his text, the evident affinities of Petrarch's collection are rather to the large number of Renaissance collections of lyric poems for which it serves as prototype. The two works are further separated by a radical difference of modality: while the *Vita Nuova* is the earliest Italian example of *prosimetrum*, a combination of poems and prose whose best-known medieval antecedents were didactic Latin texts, the *Canzoniere* contains no connective tissue of narrative and is composed of poems alone. Yet both texts are lyric collections, and both, despite their inescapable formal differences, represent an innovation in the tradition of the courtly lyric, in their assimilation of apparently discrete lyric components into an integral macrotext. In its curious combination of lyrics and prose the

Vita Nuova stands as intermediary between the lyric collections of the Duecento and the Petrarchan model of *recueil* structure whose rich posterity remains to be explored systematically. The comments that follow explore the function of the antecedent courtly lyric in the *Vita Nuova* and the *Canzoniere* as a particular question of intertextuality, that of the protogeneric narrative pattern of the poet-lover in the courtly tradition.

The precedent in vernacular literature frequently cited for the explanatory prose of the *Vita Nuova* is that of the *vidas* and *razos*, narrative accounts of the lives of Provençal poets or of the circumstances of composition of a given poem, which frequently accompanied manuscript collections of troubadour lyrics. This process of signification, as Paul Zumthor points out, involves a narrative reconstruction of the lyric enunciation in which the first-person pronoun is transposed into an objectified third person with a proper name, and the modulations of the first-person discourse are given a temporal dimension as circumstance.[1] The *vidas* and the explanations offered by the *razos*, however, differ fundamentally in function from the prose of the *Vita Nuova* in that they are not offered as validation by the author of the poems himself. In the *Vita Nuova* the opening declaration of the narrator that he is recording selectively from his own "Book of Memory" situates the narrative as autobiography, and through the narrative Dante performs on his own collection of lyrics the operation of "linear interpretation" which was carried out by compilers of troubadour texts.

As a consequence, in the *Vita Nuova* the process of objectification of lyric content is not carried out, as in the

Provençal *razos*, through transformation of the lyric "I"
into a narrative "other"; instead, the positions of love
poets implicit in the lyric tradition of the poems are made
explicit through dramatization in the life of the poet-nar-
rator.[2] Barbara Nolan describes the poet's living through
"the art of the new literary style in the drama of his own
historical actions," and the conventional nature of these
positions, their reflection of predetermined thematic and
stylistic schema crystallized in the literary tradition of the
Duecento is generally acknowledged.[3] The narrative account of the love experience of the young poet in the text
conforms to major moments of amatory and poetic experience conventionalized in the courtly lyric tradition: the
innamoramento, the resulting sense of alienation from the
uncomprehending crowd, the necessity of secrecy concerning the identity of the beloved lady, the confusion
occasioned by the curious who seek, not always sympa-
thetically, to learn the lover's secret, the alternation of
ecstasy and despair, all assume a narrative coherence in the
prose account of the early phase of the poet's love for Beatrice. Although the narrator-scribe asserts the primacy of
the poems upon which he performs the operation of glossing with prose, the radical innovation of the *Vita Nuova* is
the systematic testing of the sentiments and solutions proclaimed in the poems in terms of a life experience directly
attested in the prose.

The tradition of earlier love poetry is further evoked in
the *Vita Nuova* in the testament of poetic initiation and
maturation on the part of the protagonist. The prose valo-
rization of the poems is not effected simply through pro-
nouncements on the part of the scribe, but rather through

a coherent story of the poet's attempt to coordinate his affective experience and his poetic vocation, and for that vocation the tradition itself is the essential context. In the opening poem he salutes the *fedeli d'Amore* and submits his versified account of a compelling but obscure vision of Love and Beatrice to "many who were famous poets at that time." The postulation of an audience for the speaker's utterance, often invoked explicitly within the poems, itself conforms to a courtly lyric convention, but the prose that follows insists upon the literal intent of this appeal, recording that many poets responded with interpretations. Its further report, that none properly understood at that time the vision of Love they were asked to interpret, affords an initial suggestion of the inadequacy of that traditional audience, and throughout the *Vita Nuova* the progressive expansion of the audience for the poems suggests the evolution of the conception of love poetry itself. Major poems or series of poems signal the poet's adoption of traditional postures in the poetic expression of his personal love experience; yet the expressive function of the lyrics is repeatedly subsumed within the structured momentum of the narrative, which acknowledges the inherent limitations of successively adopted modes.[4]

Petrarch's *Canzoniere* resembles the *Vita Nuova* both in offering a collection of lyrics retrospectively arranged by their author and in the pervasive and sometimes studied utilization of the formal and thematic conventions of earlier poetry.[5] While his tribute to many of his vernacular predecessors was ready and generous, Petrarch's relative silence concerning Dante's poetry and his reported attempt to avoid even unwitting imitation of the older poet have

become increasingly suspect as a result of recent studies.[6]
Robert Durling states that "although Petrarch's wide fa-
miliarity with troubadour poetry is evident on every page
of the *Rime sparse*, the way in which he assimilated and
made use of its influence—at all levels—was shaped by the
example of Dante."[7] This formative influence, readily
documented in individual lyrics, is not less decisive in the
arrangement of the collection. On the level of *recueil* structure, Petrarch adopts from the *Vita Nuova* the "story line"
or fiction which subtends the organization of his lyric
moments—those *fragmenta* or *rime sparse* to which he refers—within a coherent macrotext.

The *Canzoniere* stands in immediate contrast to Dante's
early text in its complete absence of prose commentary.
Yet C. S. Lewis, as Durling reminds us, once wrote that
"Petrarch invented the sonnet sequence by omitting the
prose narrative found in the *Vita Nuova*,"[8] and this pro-
nouncement, despite its superficially simplistic note, suggests a process of transformation in narrative function
between the two texts. In the absence of explicit narrative
in the *Canzoniere*, the careful sequential arrangement of the
poems provokes the reader's identification of a temporal
continuity of events in the life of a single protagonist
throughout the collection, in a first-person "story" whose
coherence depends not on its possible and occasional correspondence to events in the life of the historical Petrarch
but rather on its function in the *Canzoniere* as literary text.[9]
And the "story line" that emerges from this careful patterning presents inescapable resemblances to the narrative
materia of the *Vita Nuova*: the young poet's love for an un-
attainable lady; the evolution of his youthful poetry

through his attempts to express his emotion and to praise her; his loss of her through her early death and the renewal of his praise and devotion after her death; and, throughout, his attempt to understand the intimations of this love experience for his moral and spiritual destiny. That the experience recorded emerges as meaningful rather than random, while dependent on complex internal systems of formal and thematic coordination which have yet to be explored fully, again reflects a fundamental assumption of the *Vita Nuova*: that while the poems express immediate intimate experience, the meaning of that experience is revealed only retrospectively and repeatedly qualified. In the *Canzoniere* the implicit or occasionally explicit commentary of the protagonist on the record of his past experience invests the sequential arrangement of the lyrics with further significance: with the passing of time and the accretion of additional moments of experience, both the larger pattern of his experience and its meaning are gradually disclosed.

The *Canzoniere*, like the *Vita Nuova*, is a poet's story, and the systematic evocation of the courtly lyric tradition establishes an essential referential context for the poet's discovery of his own unique poetic vocation.[10] In the selection and arrangement of his own vernacular lyrics Petrarch is adopting the same posture relative to the earlier lyric tradition as that of Dante in the compilation of the *Vita Nuova*. Each poet initially identifies his own literary enterprise through an appeal to a traditional audience, and in each work a complex network of allusions signals the poet's participation in the tradition of his predecessors. Like Dante's address to the *fedeli d'Amore*, the *Canzoniere* identifies from the proemial sonnet its vernacular audience of love initiates. In canzone 70, the most direct of the poet's signals to the reader concerning the relevance of earlier love poetry to his own practice, each stanza concludes with a verse directly quoted from an earlier love poet. The selection itself—of verses from canzoni by a poet whom Petrarch thought to be Arnaut Daniel, and also by Cavalcanti, Dante, and Cino—identifies major lines of literary relationship, but more important is its direct evocation of the varying poetic accounts of love experience offered by his predecessors, and the implicit commentary on its relevance to his own love experience as he attempts to record it in verse. In evidence of the continuity that the poem itself exemplifies, the final stanza closes with the opening verse of Petrarch's own canzone 23, also about poetry, with which, as critics have remarked, the poet of the *Canzoniere* situates himself with regard to an idealized summary of the amorous lyric tradition.[11] Petrarch does not construct an autobiographical prose fiction to bind the lyric moments of his text in narrative affirmation; yet in the sequential and thematic organization of the poems the integrative model of the young lover-poet who retrospectively assesses his experience in terms of the formal modes and affective postures of earlier poets is present as a narrative substratum in the macrotext.

While the prose account of the *Vita Nuova* suggests the fundamental narrative configuration of the *Canzoniere*, it is also to Dante's text that Petrarch's collection stands ultimately in contrast. As Dante's total absorption with Beatrice leads gradually beyond Beatrice to God, pointing to the heavenly beatitude of which her earthly presence was but a transient manifestation, so his poetic *materia* is progressively adapted to his new awareness, evolving from praise of a beloved lady to witness to a literally miraculous presence, and finally to celebration of Beatrice glorified. Following the death of Laura in the *Canzoniere*, the attempt to transcend personal loss through a poetry that raises commemoration and celebration of the beloved to the function of witness is intermittently suggested. Yet it is soon abandoned, and momentary consolation is derived from the poet's imaginative evocation of Laura's physical presence, in which the reappearance of courtly erotic imagery suggests the persistence of an earthly passion.[12] This solution of willing self-deception is unstable, however, alternating with moments of self-castigation and of despair;[13] and in the crisis occasioned by the death of Laura, her central image is progressively displaced by a complex interplay of conflicting impulses whose center is the helplessness of the poet's own state—a displacement that culminates in the apparent renunciation of the concluding *Canzone alla Vergine*.

The reader's awareness of the principles of thematic structure in a text is ultimately defined, as Barbara Smith suggests, "by his growing perception of how the work itself is generated," a perception that "forms a kind of running hypothesis which the reader constantly tests against the actual development of the work, which is ultimately confirmed (or not) by its conclusion."[14] This process of "retrospective patterning" is particularly pertinent to the terminal segment of both the *Vita Nuova* and the *Canzoniere*: in each the reader perceives an ultimate reassessment of the poet's love experience and, at the same time, of his efforts to present that experience in verse. At the end of Dante's *libello*, following a sonnet in which his spirit is raised to Heaven, where it observes his lady, the poet relates a marvelous vision that prompts him to say no more of this lady until he may one day treat adequately of her glorious state. His hope that his soul may rise "to see the glory of its lady" recalls the "glorious lady of my mind" of the opening sonnet, and at the end of the work the poet of the epilogue rejoins the scribe of the first chapter, speaking beyond the audience in the text with the solemn announcement to the reader of a work in progress. Petrarch's final canzone stands in clear opposition to this confirmation of an integrative model of love experience, poetry, and ultimate salvation. In contrast to Dante's renewed dedication to Beatrice in glory, it celebrates the type of the glorified woman, the Virgin herself, and his earthly love experience is depicted as an ever-recurring cycle from which the weary poet declares himself unable to escape without divine aid. The emphasis in the final chapter of the *Vita Nuova* on the name of "quella benedetta Beatrice" has no equivalent in Petrarch's canzone, from which Laura's name is conspicuously absent.

The narrative pattern of the aspiring poet-lover thus accommodates in the *Canzoniere* a conclusion antithetical to that of the *Vita Nuova*. That this conclusion is deliberately divergent and not merely different is confirmed in the final canzone: in the absence of Laura's name, the names of Beatrice and Medusa appear in an opposition of function which recalls their respective roles in Dante's poetry. The invocation of the Virgin as the "vera beatrice" suggests that Petrarch's earthly Laura was not a Beatrice, that her effect had been rather that of the Medusa, who had turned the now-repentant poet to stone.[15] This uncapitalized inclusion of the name of Dante's beloved is in turn profoundly ambiguous, as John Freccero has noted: it not only suggests the association of Laura with Beatrice as objects of a poet's love and devotion, but also, through urging that the Virgin is the only true mediatrix, points to the problem of idolatry, which, in Petrarch's apparent view, subtends the transformation of the courtly lady potentially present in the courtly lyric and effected in the *Vita Nuova*.[16]

With this negative assessment of the effects of Petrarch's love of Laura, a conclusion for the collection in which the praise of the earthly lady is integrated with the poet's highest spiritual aspirations is necessarily excluded.[17] Yet the poet's story in the *Canzoniere*, like that of the *Vita Nuova*, closes with an ambitious project for poetic renewal in which Petrarch's desire to enter into poetic competition with his great predecessor is confirmed. As the Virgin of the canzone is set in opposition to the earthly beloved, the hyperbolic language of courtly love is similarly afforded a corrective and a purgation through its consecration to an authentically divine love objct.[18] With the renunciation of Laura his poetic effort is rededicated, along with his love, to the Virgin, whom he prominently invokes as the new inspiration for a poetry of praise and celebration. As a consequence his future poetic achievement is to depend not on a glorified woman of his own experience but on the Virgin herself. In this program for new poetic endeavor, divinely inspired, Petrarch proposes a solution rivaling the conclusion of Dante's *Vita Nuova*, one which he perceives as a further step in transcending the limits of secular love poetry.

NOTES

1. Paul Zumthor, *Langue, texte, énigme* (Paris: Seuil, 1975), p. 178.

2. For a full discussion of Dante's use of poetic predecessors, see Charles Singleton, *An Essay on the Vita Nuova* (Cambridge: Harvard University Press, 1958). See also Gianfranco Contini, "Dante come personaggio-poeta della *Commedia*," in *Varianti e altra linguistica* (Turin: Einaudi, 1970), esp. p. 357.

3. Barbara Nolan, "The *Vita Nuova*: Dante's Book of Revelation," *Dante Studies* 88 (1970): 62; see, for example, Mariateresa Cattaneo's introductory comments to *Francesco Petrarca e la lirica d'arte del '200* (Turin: Loescher, 1964), p. xi, and the recent observations of Michelangelo Picone, "Strutture poetiche e strutture prosastiche nella *Vita Nuova*," *Modern Language Notes* 92 (1977): 127–28.

4. On poetic "occasions" and the function of the audience, see in particular Marianne Shapiro, "Society and the Theme of Praise in the *Vita Nuova*," *Neophilologus* 57 (1973): 330–40. For a detailed study of the coordination of narrative and poetic patterns in the text, see Sara Sturm-Maddox, "The Pattern of Witness: Narrative Design in the *Vita Nuova*," *Forum Italicum* 12 (1978): 216–32.

5. For a recent study suggesting that Petrarch's use of rhyme has "a strategic importance in the composition and organization of the poems" see Joseph A. Barber, "Rhyme Scheme Patterns in Petrarch's *Canzoniere*," *Modern Language Notes* 92 (1977): 139–46.

6. See in particular, M. Santagata, "Presenze di Dante 'comico' nel *Canzoniere* del Petrarca," *Giornale storico della letteratura italiana* 146 (1969): 163–211.

7. Robert Durling, *Petrarch's Lyric Poems* (Cambridge: Harvard University Press, 1976), p. 9. Durling, along with other scholars, has paid particular attention to the influence of Dante's *rime petrose*: "The way Petrarch learned to adapt to his own purposes what he found in the *rime petrose* was a key moment in the clarification of his attitude toward both the *Vita Nuova* and the *Commedia*."

8. Ibid., p. 10: "It ought to be kept in mind that, as Wilkins established, before the *Rime sparse* it was the custom to keep different metrical forms separated, in different sections of manuscripts." Durling suggests that Petrarch's positioning of canzoni or groups of canzoni "as structural nodes or pillars at varying intervals among the short poems" derives also from the *Vita Nuova* (p. 11).

9. Adelia Noferi refers to a "pseudo-narrazione"; see "Il Canzoniere del Petrarca: scrittura del desiderio e desiderio della scrittura," *Paragone letteratura* 296 (1974): 13; M. Santagata discusses the "tessuto narrativo" in "Connessioni intertestuali nel *Canzoniere* del Petrarca," *Strumenti critici* (1975), p. 139.

10. For the pattern of fictional autobiography, see Sara Sturm, "The Poet-Persona in the *Canzoniere*," in A. Scaglione, ed., *Francis Petrarch, Six Centuries Later*, Studies in the Romance Languages and Literatures, no. 159 (Chapel Hill: University of North Carolina Press, 1975), pp. 192–212.

11. See Cattaneo, pp. v–xii.

12. See Jill Tilden, "Spiritual Conflict in Petrarch's Canzoniere," in F. Schalk, ed., *Petrarca 1304–1374: Beiträge zu Werk und Wirkung* (Frankfurt am Main: Klostermann, 1975), pp. 308–9: "Her *atto dolce honesto*, her *humiltà* and the blessedness that shines out to others make of her a stilnovistic madonna, the earthly Laura placed against a painted backdrop of heaven—not the transformation of Laura into pure spirit."

13. For the opposition of this self-deception to the sublima-

tion of beauty in the stilnovistic tradition, see Oscar Büdel, "Illusion Disabused: A Novel Mode in Petrarch's *Canzoniere*," in A. Scaglione, ed., *Francis Petrarch, Six Centuries Later*, pp. 128–51.

14. Barbara H. Smith, *Poetic Closure* (Chicago: University of Chicago Press, 1968), p. 119.

15. See Kenelm Foster, "Beatrice or Medusa," in Brand, Foster, Limentani, eds., *Italian Studies Presented to E. R. Vincent* (Cambridge: at the University Press, 1962), pp. 42–56.

16. John Freccero, "The Fig Tree and the Laurel: Petrarch's Poetics," *Diacritics* 5 (1975): 40.

17. In the formally more ambitious *Trionfi*, Laura inspires her admirer during an allegorical otherworld journey on which he beholds her apotheosis.

18. Umberto Bosco observes that "alla Vergine, nella canzone finale, il Petrarca gira ad una ad una tutte le lodi di Laura;" *Francesco Petrarca* (Bari: Laterza, 1968), p. 67. See Tilden, pp. 313–14.

How Criseyde Falls in Love

JOHN M. BOWERS

C. S. Lewis does well to remind us that "at his most characteristic, medieval man was not a dreamer nor a wanderer. He was an organiser, a codifier, a builder of systems,"[1] and these systems were applied to the homely universe of human emotion as well as to the loftier houses where Love moves the sun and the other stars. Theologians, physicians, and poets alike turned their attentions to the psychology of love, its outside causes, its physiological effects, its operations within the faculties of the brain, and, if necessary, its medical cures. Andreas Capellanus, despite all the urbane burlesque of his treatise *De Amore*, confirms a common medieval understanding when he defines love as "an inborn suffering derived from the sight of and the excessive meditation upon the beauty of the opposite sex."[2] So essential is this visual experience to the inception of love that, according to Andreas, a blind man cannot love because he "cannot see anything upon which his mind can reflect immoderately."[3] The process by which the image of the lady enters through the eyes of the lover and is imprinted on his mind was analyzed by the troubadours, allegorized by Guillaume de Lorris in *Le Roman de la Rose*,[4] and repeated with textbook precision in Book I of Chaucer's *Troilus and Criseyde*: the Trojan prince sees Criseyde in the temple of Pallas, engraves her image in his mind, and then goes back to the privacy of the palace to indulge in an immoderate meditation.[5]

But the edifice of medieval doctrine, buttressed by stacks of learned treatises, was rocked whenever confronted by a profound mystery, and none was so common and vexing as the mystery of human love. While most men fall in love the way Troilus does, in real life as well as in literature,[6] this is not the way all people were known to have fallen in love—and this is not the way Criseyde falls in love. An alternate paradigm is at work, one exemplified in the charming biography of the twelfth-century Provençal poet Jaufre Rudel. According to an early *vida* repeated by Petrarch and others, Jaufre heard excellent reports about the Countess of Tripoli and fell in love with her, without ever having seen her. Her reputation for beauty was enough. He eventually traveled over the seas, fell ill, but was granted a glimpse of her face before he died.[7]

The path of love followed by Jaufre and the psychological process described by Andreas, though apparently opposites of one another, share one common feature: the formation of the beloved's image in the lover's mental faculty of *imaginativa*. As V. A. Kolve has pointed out, the Middle Ages understood that the imagination was continually forming visual images without the immediate aid of the eyes: through dreams, through religious visions, and through the evocative power of language[8]—in the case of Jaufre, through the reports of pilgrims returning from the East. Sir John Davies testified much later that this rarer form of love was no less potent than the familiar variety:

> Oft did I heare, oure Eyes the passage were,
> By which Love entred to assaile our hearts;

Therefore I guarded them, and voyd of feare
Neglected the defence of other parts.
Love knowing this, the usuall way forsooke;
And seeking, found a by-way by mine Eare:
At which hee entring, my Hart pris'ner tooke.[9]

It is small wonder that poets like Davies should have possessed such a keen insight into this turned-around process of love, since the evocation of beautiful images in the mind through the agency of language is so closely akin to the art and effect of poetry itself. Chaucer surely was aware of language's power to create visual images, as he demonstrates near the end of Book II of *The House of Fame* (ll. 1070–82), where the dreamer witnesses a puzzling sight: the conversion of speech into heavenly replicas of the people who had done the speaking back on earth—sounds converted into images.[10] In Book II of *Troilus*, Pandarus fills the dual role of poet and Cupid, the manipulator of language and the instigator of love. The joining of these two roles is signaled by Chaucer at the end of Book I when Pandarus unwittingly paraphrases a section from Geoffrey of Vinsauf's *Poetria Nova*; but while Geoffrey was writing about how to construct a poem, Pandarus is thinking about ways to make Criseyde fall in love with Troilus.[11]

Anyone who has studied Chaucer's transformations of *Il Filostrato* must be struck by the heightened sense of literary self-reflexiveness in Book II of *Troilus*, by the ways in which Chaucer has constructed this section of his poem out of a medley of in-set stories, songs, letters, anecdotes, and other artificial formulations of language.[12] His enlargement of Pandarus's role as go-between and crafty rhetorician explains but part of this increased literary self-reflexiveness,[13] for Chaucer has done more: he has arranged for a steady flow of images into Criseyde's mind in ways that often go beyond Pandarus's provision, though in curiously close accord with Pandarus's ends. Criseyde is part of the audience at a reading of the *Roman de Thebes*, she exchanges gossip with her uncle, she mentions the reading of saints' legends, and she listens to Antigone's song praising the joys of love. Not one of these features is found in the original text of Boccaccio.

Even without Chaucer's authorial interventions and his additions of well-timed accidents like Antigone's song, Pandarus on his own does a masterful job of manipulating Criseyde's thoughts and emotions. He immediately leads her mind away from the siege of Thebes, to the siege of Troy, and through a series of friendly stories, to the vital role played by Troilus in the defense of their beleaguered city. Pandarus offers four detailed vignettes carefully calculated to show Troilus's courage in the field and to suggest something of his manly appearance. Chaucer allows us to look into Pandarus's mind and watch him contriving his tales, gauging the growth of Criseyde's curiosity, and judging the right moment to spring his announcement. Once he has declared Troilus's love, Pandarus goes on to fill out his portrait of the young prince with two anecdotes illustrating the intensity of Troilus's love and the discretion of his character (II.507–74), both stories taking place in settings—the beautiful palace garden and the royal bedchamber—so familiar in the love poetry of the period that they are readily visualized or "imaged" in Criseyde's mind.

Although Andreas Capellanus had emphasized that a

woman ought to seek as her lover a man of excellent character and virtuous reputation,[14] a visual image still had to
be introduced into the lady's mind. Accordingly, Pandarus
has not only sung the praises of Troilus's character but has
gone far toward painting his physical image in Criseyde's
imagination. Chaucer arranges the rest. Alone and deep in a
meditation on all that her uncle has said to her, Criseyde is
roused from her reverie by noises from the street (II.610–
51). She rushes to the window in time to see Troilus passing, arrayed in his knightly arms, mounted on a bay steed,
and bearing the marks of heated battle—exactly as Pandarus had described him.

Criseyde now has her visual image of Prince Troilus and
can proceed apace toward her love and her destiny. But we
as readers and critics should pause at this point to examine
the image she has seen: Troilus on his horse. Where has
it appeared earlier in the text? And what is the range of
meaning permitted by the poem? We must make ourselves
like Chaucer's first audience, the lexicographers of his
images. The poet insists that we see Troilus the beloved in
connection with his horse, and he alters Boccaccio in order
to reinforce this association. The first two times that Criseyde sees Troilus, he is mounted on his bay (II.624–27 and
1248–49); in the first instance, Boccaccio made Troilo
walk past her house on foot,[15] while the second scene occurs nowhere in *Il Filostrato*.

Earlier in the poem, in a simile that stands as one of the
most famous additions to the original Italian, Chaucer
characterizes Troilus at the moment he falls in love as a
proud Bayard being whipped back into his tandem to follow "horses lawe" (I.218–24). This, then, is the image that

Chaucer insists upon, and as far as the psychology of the characters goes, this literal image is all that Criseyde needs to fall in love. But medieval audiences had different habits of perception responsive to centuries of insistence that seeing and especially reading were processes of intellectual inquiry and moral discovery. The strictest guides warned readers that they needed to seek the figurative significances of literary images in order to avoid spiritual blindness.[16] We can never be sure how thoroughly this injunction was carried out from age to age and from individual to individual, especially when the literature at hand was vernacular and secular, but it seems clear that certain images are presented to the reader as icons demanding some amount of interpretation. Chaucer does not compare Troilus to a horse merely for the sake of decoration.

The Trojan story itself offers considerable help in glossing this image. Everyone knew how the Trojan horse, itself a gargantuan image accepted as an offering to Pallas, had contributed to the defeat of Troy, and the verbal similarity between *Troy* and *Troilus* is too obvious to be ignored.[17] But the association between Troy and the horse goes further. Caxton, repeating earlier geographers in *The Mirrour of the World*, explains that Troy had taken for itself the emblem of a horse, suggested by the horses native to that region.[18] Troilus, the proud Bayard, therefore emerges as a carefully studied microcosm, the human embodiment of the city whose destruction was caused, according to Dante and others, by the sin of pride.[19]

Most members of Chaucer's audience would not have needed learned commentaries and historical treatises in order to understand the moral implications of the horse as

an iconographic image. D. W. Robertson, Jr., has demonstrated that the horse was often—though, I would add, not
always—a symbol of lust.[20] Poets and moralists alike used
the image of a man mounted on a horse as one way of describing, slyly perhaps, a man mounting a woman during
sexual intercourse.[21] This erotic dimension may help explain Criseyde's intense reaction when she first sees Troilus
riding by, and Chaucer seems to develop the imagery in
just this way in Book V when Troilus turns over Criseyde's bridle to Diomede (v.90–92). Later in the same
book, Chaucer goes even further in the direction of pure
symbolic communication. We are told that Criseyde presents Diomede with the bay steed he had once won from
Troilus (v.1037–39). The passage is confusing, a cause for
real puzzlement,[22] and the literal narrative offers us no clue
to the origins of this gift horse. In a figurative sense, however, it anticipates Criseyde's gift of herself to the Greek
warrior.

While Criseyde first sees Troilus mounted *on* a horse,
the audience has a different iconographic introduction: we
see him *as* a horse, the proud Bayard, and we should not
be surprised to watch him bridled, mounted, and ridden—
at least in the moral sense. The Middle Ages allowed for
this inversion of the conventional image and popularized it
in the fable of Aristotle and Phyllis. The proud philos-
opher, who had scoffed at Alexander's weakness for wom-
en (much as Troilus had rebuked his friends), fell in love
himself with the beautiful Phyllis, and in order to win her
sexual favors, he allowed himself to be bridled and ridden
like a horse. Out of sight and watching from above, King
Alexander looked on with superior amusement.[23]

While puzzling over the fact that Chaucer is associating the horse image with Troilus as well as with Criseyde—both eventually acknowledge their animal spirits—we should also notice that the poet's explicit interpretation of the icon is not what we might have expected. Bayard is primarily a proud horse, not a lustful one, and it is pride as much as love that leads Troilus to his tragic end through his stiff-necked insistence on keeping his affair secret from his friends and the rest of the court. Moralists consistently condemned pride as a form of spiritual blindness,[24] but Troilus is also affected by a more psychological form of blindness. Because his thoughts are wholly turned inward upon the literal image of Criseyde imprinted in his mind, Troilus sinks deeper and deeper into a state of amorous blindness comparable to that of Old January, who stooped beneath the pear tree to let the unfaithful May mount up on his back.[25]

As a work of fiction that wrestles with the knottiest problems of Boethian epistemology, Chaucer's *Troilus* is entangled in questions involving vision and understanding, illusion and reality, the visible and invisible foes of this world. These concerns go far beyond the ways that Troilus and Criseyde see and imagine each other as lovers. Seldom did a medieval writer delineate such an elaborate hierarchy of perspectives, so many ways for the action and its characters to be perceived. For the purposes of analogy, we might recall the extraordinary scene in Shakespeare's *Troilus and Cressida* (v.ii.) in which Troilus witnesses his beloved's infidelity: Cressida flirts with Diomedes at center stage; Troilus and Ulysses watch from above, concealed; further up, Thersites comments mockingly on all their activities; and the audience, withdrawn to the farthest distance, sees all three levels of action at once. A comparable layering of perspectives is taking place in Book II of Chaucer's poem: Troilus, conscious of his public image, rides his horse through the streets of Troy; Criseyde and Pandarus watch and discuss him as he passes the window of her house; Chaucer the narrator offers his own comments on the action; and we the audience see it all. We watch the watcher watching the watchers who watch the watched.

This multiplication of perspectives raises questions that reach to the heart of Chaucer's concept of poetry—its power to create illusions and its duty to reveal truth—and it is by way of responding to the breadth of these questions, if not to any single one, that I shall close this paper with one final consideration of my original subject, love inspired through the medium of language. While we the audience may be granted the fullest and most distanced view of the action, we are in no sense dispassionate spectators. Indeed the control of our emotions was of primary importance to the poet as well as to the playwright, though each wished us to respond differently to Calchas's daughter. While Shakespeare uses the aforementioned scene in Act V of his play to make the audience hate Cressida, Chaucer sets out in Book II of his poem to accomplish a much harder task: he wants us to fall in love with her. To achieve this end he resorts to exactly the same technique as Pandarus, by using language to engrave her womanly image in our minds.

In Book I Criseyde is little more than the eidolon of a beautiful lady Troilus had seen at the temple—attractive, feminine, graceful, the stock heroine of a hundred romances. But in Book II she becomes something quite different, a complete and fully animated woman, vulnerable, charming, witty, and just wise enough in the ways of the world. When in Book V her infidelity is nearly certain, Criseyde vanishes from the poem completely. This comes as a great blow, for us no less than for Troilus, because like him we have lost the image of the woman we have grown to love. Just as Pandarus offers no real consolation when he advises Troilus to choose another lady, Chaucer's palinode is an inadequate response to *our* sense of loss, the tonal equivalent of "She ys ded! . . . Be God, hyt ys routhe!" We come away from the poem wiser but sadder—sadder because we have been emotionally entangled in the web of a great love tragedy; and wiser because, like Troilus smiling down from the top of heaven, we too have been granted the superior perspective, a "ful avysement" of two attractive people, earthly and therefore fragile, colliding in their erratic courses through Love's lesser cosmos.

NOTES

1. C. S. Lewis, *The Discarded Image* (Cambridge: at the University Press, 1964), p. 10.

2. Andreas Capellanus, *The Art of Courtly Love*, trans. John Jay Parry (New York: W. W. Norton and Co., 1969), p. 28.

3. *The Art of Courtly Love*, p. 33.

4. D. W. Robertson, Jr., *A Preface to Chaucer: Studies in Medieval Perspectives* (Princeton: Princeton University Press, 1962),

pp. 91–98; Guillaume de Lorris and Jean de Meun, *The Romance of the Rose*, trans. and intro. by Charles Dahlberg (Princeton: Princeton University Press, 1971), pp. 15–16. Jean de Meun's story of Pygmalion (Dahlberg, ll. 20817–1214) is discussed as an allegory of this love process by Robertson, pp. 99–104, and John V. Fleming, *The Roman de la Rose: A Study in Allegory and Iconography* (Princeton: Princeton University Press, 1969), pp. 228–37.

5. *Troilus*, 1.267–392. For all Chaucerian quotations and references, see Geoffrey Chaucer, *Works*, 2d ed., ed. Fred N. Robinson (Boston: Houghton Mifflin, 1957).

6. Froissart says that Edward III, for example, had a similar reaction when he first saw the Countess of Salisbury; see *The Chronicles*, trans. Thomas Johnes (London: William Smith, 1848), vol. 1, chap. 77, pp. 102–3.

7. *Introduction à l'étude de l'ancien provençal*, ed. Frank R. Hamlin, Peter T. Ricketts, and John Hathaway (Geneva: Droz, 1967), pp. 87–88.

8. V. A. Kolve, "Chaucer and the Visual Arts," *Writers and Their Backgrounds: Geoffrey Chaucer*, ed. Derek Brewer (Athens: Ohio University Press, 1975), pp. 290–320, esp. 296 and 300–306.

9. Sir John Davies, "Upon Loves entring by his Eares," in *Poems*, ed. Robert Krueger (Oxford: Clarendon Press, 1975), p. 187.

10. For recent commentary, see Laurence K. Shook, "*The House of Fame*" in *Companion to Chaucer Studies*, ed. Beryl Rowland (London: Oxford University Press, 1968), p. 350; and A. C. Spearing, *Medieval Dream-Poetry* (Cambridge: at the University Press, 1976), p. 81.

11. *Troilus*, 1.1065–71, where Pandarus's plot is compared to the planning of a house. The source is most likely Geoffrey of Vinsauf, *Poetria Nova*, in *Les Arts poétiques du XII⁰ et du XIII⁰ siècles*, ed. Edmond Faral (1924; rpt. Paris: Honoré Champion, 1958), p. 198 (ll. 43–49). For similar ideas, including those ex-

pressed in *Boece*, IV, pr. 6, 80–96, see James J. Murphy, "A New Look at Chaucer and the Rhetoricians," *Review of English Studies*, n.s. 15 (1964): 14–15.

12. Rossell Hope Robbins suggests in "The Lyrics," *Companion to Chaucer Studies* (see n. 10 above), p. 315, that numerous lyric clusters give *Troilus* the effect of a "vast sonnet sequence." John Gardner, *The Life and Times of Chaucer* (New York: Knopf, 1977), p. 214, notes that while Petrarch and Boccaccio were trying to escape traditional "panel-structure poetry," Chaucer reasserts the medieval principle of segmentation.

13. Charles Muscatine, *Chaucer and the French Tradition: A Study in Style and Meaning* (Berkeley: University of California Press, 1957), p. 141, states that Pandarus's function as go-between is expanded beyond anything found in earlier French romances and fabliaux. Pandarus's narrative self-consciousness appears, for example, in *Troilus*, II.256–63. E. Talbot Donaldson points out that Pandarus constantly uses language to manipulate the lovers' perception of reality and to encourage their acceptance of illusions; see his *Chaucer's Poetry: An Anthology for the Modern Reader* (New York: Ronald Press, 1958), p. 972.

14. *The Art of Courtly Love*, pp. 33–34; cf. Dante, "Amore e'l cor gentil sono una cosa," ll. 9–14 in *La Vita Nuova*.

15. Giovanni Boccaccio, *Il Filostrato*, trans. Nathaniel E. Griffin and Arthur B. Myrick (Philadelphia: University of Pennsylvania Press, 1929), pp. 202–3 (II.82).

16. This caveat is forcefully expressed, for example, by Augustine, *On Christian Doctrine*, trans. D. W. Robertson, Jr. (Indianapolis: Liberal Arts Press of Bobbs-Merrill, 1958), pp. 83–84 (III.v.9).

17. John P. McCall, "The Trojan Scene in Chaucer's *Troilus*," *Journal of English Literary History* 26 (1962): 264, observes that the name Troilus means "Little Troy."

18. William Caxton, *The Mirrour of the World*, ed. Oliver H. Prior, Early English Text Society [EETS], extra series [e.s.], no. 110 (London: Oxford University Press, 1913), p. 94. Caxton's French source, *Image du monde* (ca. 1245), derived this

notion from Gervase of Tilbury, *Otia imperialia* (ca. 1211), ed.
G. G. Leibnitz, *Scriptorum Brunsvicensia*, vol. 2 (Hanover, 1710),
p. 767 (II.ix) and Honorius Augustodunensis, *De imagine mundi*,
in *Patrologia Latina*, ed. J.-P. Migne, 172: 129 (I.xxviii): "Troja
equi figuram habuit."

19. McCall, p. 263, cites Dante, *Inferno*, I.75 and XXX.13–15,
Virgil, *Aeneid*, III.1–3, and Horace, *Epistle to Maximus Lollius* in
Satires, Epistles, Ars Poetica, trans. H. Rushton Fairclough (Cambridge, Mass.: Loeb Library, 1929), p. 263. Dante also uses Troy
as an example of pride in *Purgatorio*, XII.61–63.

20. Robertson, *A Preface to Chaucer*, pp. 30, 194, 253–55,
394, and 476. This association was perpetuated by writers who
attributed extraordinary sexual energies to horses: Isidore, *Etymologiarum sive originum*, ed. W. M. Lindsay (Oxford: Clarendon Press, 1911), XII.i.41; Brunetto Latini, *Li Livres dou tresor*,
ed. Francis J. Carmody (Berkeley: University of California
Press, 1948), I.186.6 (p. 163); Bartholomaeus Anglicus, *On the
Properties of Things: John Trevisa's Translation of Bartholomaeus
Anglicus, "De Proprietatibus Rerum,"* gen. ed. M. C. Seymour,
2 vols. (Oxford: Clarendon Press, 1975), XVIII.39 (p. 1188).

21. For the classical origins of the notion of "the steeds of
passion," see David Knowles, *The Evolution of Medieval Thought*
(London: Longmans, Green and Co., 1962), p. 207. Medieval
examples are very numerous. For further discussion, see A. A.
Dent, "Chaucer and the Horse," *Proceedings of the Leeds Philosophical and Literary Society*, vol. 9, pt. 1 (1959), pp. 1–12; Beryl
Rowland, "The Horse and Rider Figure in Chaucer's Works,"
University of Toronto Quarterly 35 (1966): 246–59; and Beryl
Rowland, *Animals with Human Faces* (Knoxville: University of
Tennessee Press, 1973), pp. 103–9. Interestingly, the thought
of proud lovers mounted upon their horses led John Lydgate to
recall the tragedy of Troilus in "*Amor vincit omnia mentiris quod
pecunia,*" in *The Minor Poems: Secular Poems*, ed. Henry Noble
MacCracken, E E T S, o.s. 192 (London: Oxford University
Press, 1934), p. 745, ll. 1–22.

22. Thynne was so perplexed that he altered the passage to

read that Criseyde herself had won the steed from Troilus (Robinson, p. 835).

23. Emile Mâle, *The Gothic Image*, trans. Dora Nussey (1913; rpt. New York: Harper and Row, 1958), pp. 333–35; George Sarton, "Aristotle and Phyllis," *Isis* 14 (1930): 8–19; Raimond van Marle, *Iconographie de l'art profane au moyen-âge et à la Renaissance: Allégories et symboles* (The Hague: Martinus Nijhoff, 1932), pp. 479–95; David J. A. Ross, "Allegory and Romance on a Mediaeval French Marriage Casket," *Journal of the Warburg and Courtauld Institute* 11 (1948): 112–42; Raffaele de Cesare, *Di nuovo sulla leggenda de Aristotele cavalcato*, Pubblicazioni dell' Università Cattolica del S. Cuore, no. 58 (Milan, 1956), pp. 181–247; Raffaele de Cesare, "Miscellanea: Due recenti studi sulla leggenda di Aristotele cavalcato," *Aevum* 31 (1957): 85–101; and Rowland, *Animals with Human Faces*, p. 106. The fable is also mentioned by poets Chaucer knew: Guillaume de Machaut, *La Fonteinne amoureuse*, in *Oeuvres*, ed. Ernest Hoepffner (Paris: Librairie Ancienne Edouard Champion, 1921) 3: 207–8 (ll. 1813–44); Jean Froissart, *Le Joli Buisson de Jonece*, ed. Anthime Fourrier (Geneva: Droz, 1975), pp. 164–65 (ll. 3366–75); and John Gower, *Confessio Amantis*, in *The English Works*, ed. G. C. Macaulay, EETS, e.s. 82 (London: Oxford University Press, 1901), pp. 459–60 (VIII.2705–13).

24. See, for example, *The Book of Vices and Virtues*, ed. W. Nelson Francis, EETS, o.s. 217 (London: Oxford University Press, 1942), p. 11. For a fuller account of Troilus's blindness, see P. M. Kean, *Chaucer and the Making of English Poetry*, vol. 1: *Love Vision and Debate* (London: Routledge and Kegan Paul, 1972), pp. 151–61.

25. There are several fine studies on love's blindness and the iconography used to represent it: Erwin Panofsky, "Blind Cupid," *Studies in Iconology: Humanistic Themes in the Art of the Renaissance* (1939; rpt. New York: Harper and Row, 1972), pp. 95–128; Margaret Ann Twycross, "The Representation of the Major Classical Divinities in the Works of Chaucer, Gower,

Lydgate and Henryson" (B. Litt. thesis, Oxford, 1962), p. 339; Vinzenz Buchheit, "Amor Caecus," *Classica et Mediaevalia* 25 (1965): 129–37; C. D. Gilbert, "Blind Cupid," *Journal of the Warburg and Courtauld Institute* 33 (1970): 304–5. See also Robertson, *A Preface to Chaucer*, pp. 112, 275, 476, and 478.

Early Secular Courtly Drama in France

L'Estoire de Griseldis

DONALD MADDOX

From its twelfth-century origins the vernacular drama of medieval France occasionally reflects courtly settings, systems of values, and even the inspiration of nondramatic courtly literature. One might cite the quasifeudal terminology with which Adam addresses his Creator in the *Jeu d'Adam*, or the sporadic elements of French epic and romance that enliven Bodel's *Jeu de Saint Nicolas*, the somewhat theatrical *Aucassin et Nicolette*, and certain of the later miracle plays. Nor may we forget that lively *pastourelle par personnages, Robin et Marion*, nor the intermittent courtliness and the evident qualities of the courtly poet in Adam de la Halle's *Jeu de la feuillée* and in the *serventoys* of the *Miracles de Notre Dame*. Even the courts of the King of Heaven, or of Herod, or of Pilate, as evoked in the mysteries, bear numerous resemblances to royal and feudal courts. Yet despite the many courtly aspects of these and other early plays during the first two centuries of vernacular drama in France, we find scant evidence of close adaptation of plays from the wealth of available secular courtly works.[1] One of the earliest and perhaps also the most faithful of direct adaptations from an identifiable narrative model in courtly literature is *L'Estoire de Griseldis*, written in 1395 and probably first presented at the court of King Charles VI of France.[2]

L'Estoire de Griseldis is based on the story of low-born Griselda, renowned for her wifely patience in spite of the cruel tests of obedience imposed upon her by her noble husband, as he deprives her one at a time of their two children and later pretends to annul their marriage so that he may wed a noblewoman. The story has long been associated with possible antecedents in folklore, notably with the "patience group" of tales stemming from the story of Cupid and Psyche.[3] Yet the earliest-known literary version of the story appears in 1353, only forty-two years before the play, as the last novella (Giornata X, Novella 10) in Boccaccio's *Decameron*. Within less than a half-century, the story had been retold at least four times, first in 1373 by Petrarch in his famous Latin prose adaptation of Boccaccio's version, by Chaucer in his *Clerkes Tale*, written after 1380, as well as in two French prose translations of Petrarch's account, one of which is by Philippe de Mézières.[4] It has been shown that Mézières's version (ca. 1384–89) is the immediate source from which over two-thirds of the play's octosyllabic verses have been closely refashioned, and Grace Frank has even argued that Mézières himself is the probable author of the play as well as of its prose source.[5]

With respect to its narrative antecedents, the 2604 verses of the play constitute not only a transformation of material from one medium to another but an expansion and an elaboration of the tradition as well. In *The Literary Relations of Chaucer's Clerke's Tale*, J. Burke Severs has traced the late fourteenth-century literary development of the story from the reminiscences of folktale and "the worldly, somewhat licentious" tone of Boccaccio's last novella, through the rhetorical amplifications and the "elevated, moral, almost pious point of view" of Petrarch's version, to the additions and expansions made by Philippe de Mézières in his prose reworking of the Petrarchan model.[6] Although borrowing freely from Mézières's prose, the playwright has likewise added to the traditional material, providing hunting scenes, shepherd scenes, and two depictions of childbirth, and creating a host of new roles, mostly at the court of Griseldis's husband Gautier, the Marquis de Saluces. From Boccaccio's closing novella to the play, then, we observe the progressive metamorphoses of the story of Griselda, as its folk substratum, most evident in the *Decameron*, is gradually overlaid with elements that heighten its ethical and social coherence and is finally cast into dramatic form.

The courtly nature of the play's immediate literary sources is apparent in the 100-verse prologue, which sets forth the circumstances leading up to the wedding of Gautier and Griseldis.[7] We learn that in the Italian Piedmont, Gautier is the lord of all other marquis, barons, knights, squires, bourgeois, and merchants, all of whom obey him (vv. 55–60). His physical and moral portrait is nearly flawless, yet he devotes all of his time to hawking and hunting instead of governing his subjects and had avoided the bonds of matrimony until convinced by his barons that he must marry and provide an heir to his realm.

In addition to the organization of society around the court of the marquis and the motivation of his marriage by courtiers who wish to assure the court's future, the courtly dimension in the prose background of the play recalls elements found in early courtly romances. A brief comparison of Mézières's prose version and the *Erec et Enide* of Chrétien de Troyes will suffice to reveal a few of these characteristics. As in the first part of *Erec*, hunting and hawking form a thematic background against which the noble protagonist negotiates the terms of his marriage with the father of a poorly clad maiden who tends livestock. Despite her poverty, the maiden's behavior reveals courtly refinements, and she is depicted as a mirror in which one might see oneself reflected.[8] Her appearance is enhanced as she is made to doff her humble attire and don a splendid gown tailored to the body of a lady at court.[9] In both works the wedding occurs at court and the bride is conveyed on a special mount.[10] In the second part of each work, where we may contrast Enide's broken silences and persistent though loyal disobedience with Griseldis's unflagging obedience, there is the prominent theme of testing, whereby the husband at some point discloses that earlier circumstances have been a test that the wife has completed successfully.[11] In *Erec* the reconciliation of the couple with each other and with courtly society is marked by the "Joy of the Court" episode and celebrated in the sumptuous coronation, while the prose tradition celebrates the reunion of the marquis and his wife and the return of their children amidst the joyful assembly of a plenary court. This is not to imply the direct influence of *Erec* or of any other courtly romance on the prose stories of Griselda, nor even to suggest any commonly shared background in folklore, but merely to show how the prose tradition from which the play derives blends folk motifs with a courtly context in a manner akin to that of earlier courtly romances. As we turn to the play, we must bear in mind these secondary courtly elements derived from the prose tradition in order to recognize the primary courtly elements added by the playwright himself.

First among these additions is the aforementioned prologue, which has much in common with the prologues of courtly romance. There is a clear statement of the twofold intention to delight and to edify; the author alludes to the inherent truth and value of his source and expresses his desire to recast it so as to enhance its instructive features.[12] He twice presents his subject according to the "memorability topos" (vv. 1–10; 45–46): the story's qualities make it worthy of retelling and thus recording for posterity.[13] A further courtly element, perhaps of more recent vintage, stems from the playwright's explanation of what prompted him to transform his source from prose to play. We are told that man may "rise to a state of perfection" (vv. 20–21) by hearing an exemplary narration but that the story of Griseldis will be dramatized—"fait par personnages" (v. 30)—because the heart of man is even more readily moved by seeing than by simply hearing. We find the same sensory doctrine, according to which the involvement of two higher senses—hearing and seeing—is superior to that of only one, in the late fourteenth-century *Livres du roy Modus et de la royne Ratio* (ca. 1354–76) by Henri de Ferrières.[14] In this comprehensive, heavily allegorized handbook on hunting, that noblest of all medieval pastimes, an *altercatio* between hunters and falconers over which is the more pleasurable sport culminates in a long, versified courtly debate by two noblewomen, one of whom argues the superiority of the stag hunt while the other praises hunting with sparrow hawks. Their arguments are submitted to the Count of Tancarville, who rules in favor of hunting the stag because it is a spectacle pleasing to both eye and ear while hawking affords only visual delight.[15]

Whether the playwright's sensory theory of drama as an instructive medium stems directly from the aesthetic views set forth in this contemporary treatise on the techniques and moral significance of hunting is an open question. Yet in view of the play's two original hunting scenes, one an engaging episode of falconry and the other a spirited chase for the stag complete with hounds, there can be no doubt that the playwright was well acquainted with the formal aspects of hawking and hunting as set forth in treatises like the *Modus*.

These two hunting scenes, neither of which occurs in the prose versions, serve to motivate and explain Gautier's bizarre testing of his wife.[16] At the beginning of the play the two hunting scenes frame the decisive encounter between Gautier and the Quint Chevalier, an elderly and venerable figure created by the playwright to express the desire of Gautier's subjects that he marry and provide an heir. Because of this obligation, Gautier consents to marry but voices his fear that marriage will force him to forego the pleasures of hunting, to lose his freedom, and to become effeminate at heart (vv. 354–77). This speech recalls the question frequently entertained in courtly romance concerning the proper relationship of prowess and conjugal love. So long as prowess is maintained apart from marriage it is nonproblematic. Yet as Chrétien de Troyes had shown in *Erec et Enide* and *Yvain* over two centuries earlier, the married warrior or hunter must strive to maintain his prowess in order to avoid the pitfall of *recréantise*, or cowardice.[17] Gautier's fear that marriage necessarily precludes hunting and therefore threatens to diminish his masculinity suggests that he is aware of the sort of problem set forth by Chrétien and would prefer to avoid it. Although he is assured by the Quint Chevalier that in marriage the male is dominant (vv. 420–23), Gautier's subsequent behavior with regard to marriage betrays his reluctance to forsake hunting as his primary model of dominance and control.

On the day designated for his wedding, but before he has chosen a bride, Gautier requests information about a nearby shepherdess from his huntsman, who now reports the condition of unsuspecting Griseldis before her wedding (vv. 752–77), just as he had reported the condition of the stag before the chase (vv. 642–45, 648–53). This implicit metaphor equating Griseldis with the game in Gautier's preserve recalls the ominously sexual image of the heron soaring above the river as it falls prey to Gautier's falcon—

> Vostre faulcon a ja saisi
> Le hairon et mis dessoubz lui.
> Si fault aler querre la proye.*
> [vv. 145–47]

—just as Griseldis will soon become the hunter's wife and, in a sense, his prey. In marriage, however, one does not dominate one's mate with falcons and hounds; some other means must be found to measure sovereignty. Thus, for

---

*Your falcon has already seized the heron and gotten it beneath him. We must now go and seek the prey.

Gautier, testing becomes a kind of surrogate for hawking and hunting, for it enables the married hunter to gain the same sense of control over his obedient wife that he once held over his prey in hunting. By magnifying Gautier's zest for hunting, the playwright has suggested a coherent explanation of the marquis's strange behavior in all versions of the story; the extensive depiction of this courtly *deduit* is an effective means of revealing Gautier's attempt to manage his domestic life with the same degree of sovereignty he formerly maintained through field and stream. Yet, like Saint Eustache in the legend, Gautier unwittingly becomes the hunter hunted, won over by the steadfast love exhibited by his prey.

In the play the recurrent allusions to the effects of fortune on the life of the court heighten the intensity of Gautier's desire to maintain total control. He justifies his separation from Griseldis and planned remarriage with the false implication that "unstable fortune" has decreed his subjects' alleged preference that he marry a noblewoman (vv. 2067–93), and one of his barons even curses fortune for having thus disrupted the court (vv. 2180–81). It is nevertheless Gautier and not fortune who has arranged the unhappy circumstances at court. By striving to maintain a precarious sense of control over the misfortunes of his wife, he seeks to place himself above the accidents of fortune. Yet a lady of the court perceptively remarks that "unhappy is she who relies on such unstable nobility" (vv. 2198–99). This is typical of the manner in which the many secondary characters in the play, most of whom are barons, knights, and ladies at Gautier's court, provide a normative social context and serve as a chorus to reflect upon the events. These many courtly roles provide a solid point of identification from which the spectator may better understand certain circumstances that lack adequate commentary in previous versions. Knights and ladies at court repeatedly comment on the strange behavior of the marquis or the remarkable refinement and patience of Griseldis.[18] For the poor maidens as for one of the shepherds of the two lengthy *bergeries* that close each of the two "acts" of the drama, Griseldis represents their hopes for upward social mobility (vv. 1015–38, 1113–16), while the other shepherd severely upbraids his companion for wanting to become a knight and convinces him of the superior virtues of simple rustic life (vv. 1195–1224).[19] Likewise, Janicola, the father of Griseldis, deplores the vanity and mutability of "jeunes seigneurs" and counsels his daughter to remain indifferent to fortune and rely on the love of God (vv. 2265–71). Indeed, his daughter's patient acceptance of the vicissitudes of her life is what causes Gautier to soften and relinquish his tyrannical drive to control.

Yet in the play, by virtue of the detailed depiction of the court, she is more than an emblem of extreme conjugal fidelity. The knight who sees her as a heavenly emissary sent for the salvation of the "bien publique" recognizes the collective nature of her role, for she in fact becomes the mediatory agent by whom the reintegration of the court is effected.[20] By her indifference to her station in life, whether in a noble palace or the paternal hovel, she provides an instructive model of cheerful constancy in adversity to which all sectors of courtly society respond, whence her universal appeal as a mediatrix of prowess and love, forest and hearth, poverty and wealth. At the marquis's closing plenary court, the largest ever assembled (vv. 2534–35), Griseldis becomes the nucleus around whom is crystallized a newly integrated society in which the hierarchy of social classes remains as before, but in harmonious recognition of the potential of human qualities that transcend them all in the communal joy of the court.

There is evidence that the playwright sought to heighten the collective dimension by creating a play structured symmetrically so as to emphasize the two plenary spectacles, the wedding and the closing festive reunion. In contrast with prose antecedents, the play features a more emphatic bipartite structure not unlike those found in the courtly romance. In earlier versions of the story of Griselda, the events leading up to the wedding normally occupy no more than a third of the text, whereas the playwright has augmented the early episodes prior to the marriage so that they occupy nearly half of the total verses.[21] Moreover, both the wedding at the end of the first half of the play and the final scene of the plenary court are closed by *bergeries*, while the pattern of mnemonic rhyme, where the first line of a speech forms a couplet with the last line of the preceding speech, in use throughout the play, nevertheless culminates in a rhymed couplet at the end of each *bergerie*, thus creating the effect of a play having two distinct acts. Likewise, the division also recalls the bipartite courtly narrative, where the achievement of equilibrium in an initial movement is disrupted by some unforeseen element that necessitates a second search for renewed and lasting stability. A common example of bipartition is the "bride-winning" pattern, whereby a hero wins a bride but for some reason must repeat a new variant of the pattern before closure occurs.

In the play the search for a bride culminates in marriage and communal joy at court, only to be disrupted by the cruel disappearance of the couple's children and their own separation prior to the final recognition and joyful reunion at court. Thus, bipartition lends a new symmetry to the play while recapturing the twofold rhythm of dysphoria and euphoria typical of many courtly romances.

The French play of *Griseldis* frequently has been treated as an anomaly in the history of medieval French drama. It cannot be identified with earlier types of serious drama, such as the mystery, miracle, or morality play, for, unlike these, it does not rely on either biblical or hagiographic material or on religious allegory. Yet it is not the curious hybrid that one might be tempted to identify by considering it primarily in terms of its reminiscences of earlier drama. Apart from creating a greater historical sense of the play's unique characteristics, it is hardly worthwhile to characterize it in terms of its possible generic relationships to earlier French *plays*, for it is clearly not a miracle of the Virgin minus Our Lady, nor a modified Christmas play retaining only the birth scenes and shepherds, nor a descendant of the Bodelian saint's play because of its prologue, nor even a morality play without the allegory.[22] While the playwright benefited technically from the traditions of religious drama, it is evident from comparisons of the play with earlier narrative versions that his aim was not to implement antecedent types of religious drama for the realization of a secular play, but rather to develop dramatic potential latent in the courtly prose tradition. In view of these circumstances, *L'Estoire de Griseldis* is in effect a courtly play in two major senses of the term. While its subject is derived entirely from a specific courtly narrative, the play is also focused exclusively on the constituents and problems of a specific court portrayed within a totally secular context. We may therefore modify its earlier anomalous status by identifying it as the first known instance of a secular French play that is both courtly and of the court.

NOTES

1. The intertextual rapport of *Robin et Marion* with a courtly poetic genre would seem to constitute a notable exception. See Michel Zink, *La Pastourelle: Poésie et folklore au moyen âge* (Paris: Bordas, 1972), pp. 104–5. Yet *Robin et Marion* is not merely a dramatized *pastourelle*. Its augmentations represent a considerable departure from the simpler format of the *pastourelle*.

2. See Marie-Anne Glomeau, ed., *Le Mystère de Griseldis* (Paris: Maurice Glomeau, 1923), pp. xv–xvi; Grace Frank, "The Authorship of *Le Mystère de Griseldis*," *Modern Language Notes* 51 (1936): 217–22; and Barbara M. Craig, ed., *L'Estoire de Griseldis* (Lawrence: University of Kansas Press, 1954), pp. 4–8.

3. See Dudley D. Griffith, *The Origin of the Griselda Story*, University of Washington Publications in Language and Literature, vol. 8, no. 1 (Seattle, 1931); W. A. Cate, "The Problem of the Origin of the Griselda Story," *Studies in Philology* 29 (1932): 389–405; and Craig, pp. 1–3.

4. To this list we must add an Italian version by Giovanni Sercambi (ca. 1374), condensed from Boccaccio's version. For a complete account of versions of the Griselda story in the fourteenth century, see J. Burke Severs, *The Literary Relations of Chaucer's Clerke's Tale* (New Haven: Yale University Press, 1942), pp. 3–37. Elie Golenistcheff-Koutouzoff has identified

the French prose version by Philippe de Mézières in *L'histoire de Griseldis en France au XIVe et au XVe siècle* (Paris: E. Droz, 1933), pp. 42–43.

5. See Golenistcheff-Koutouzoff, p. 120; Severs, pp. 29–31; Frank, "Authorship"; Craig, p. 8.

6. Severs, pp. 12–29.

7. This prologue contains numerous passages derived from *Le Livre de la vertu et du sacrement de mariage et du reconfort des dames mariées*, the treatise on marriage which has been attributed to P. de Mézières. See Golenistcheff-Koutouzoff, pp. 34–35, 157–58; Craig, pp. 3–4.

8. Mézières's version is in Golenistcheff-Koutouzoff, pp. 153–82. Cf. Mario Roques, ed., *Les Romans de Chrétien de Troyes*, vol. 1: *Erec et Enide*, Classiques Français du Moyen Age [CFMA], no. 80 (Paris: H. Champion, 1952), vv. 437–41: "Que diroie de sa biauté? / Ce fu cele por verité / qui fu fete por esgarder, / qu'an se poïst an li mirer / ausi com an un mireor." Cf. "Le Miroir des dames mariées," the title given the story of Griseldis in *Le Livre de la vertu* and echoed by the dramatist's prologue (vv. 7–14).

9. Cf. *Erec*, vv. 1562–72, and Golenistcheff-Koutouzoff, pp. 160–61.

10. Cf. Enide's palfrey in *Erec*, vv. 1360–86, and Golenistcheff-Koutouzoff, pp. 164, 201.

11. Cf. *Erec*, vv. 4882–93, and Golenistcheff-Koutouzoff, p. 179.

12. "D'une dame la vraye histoire, / Qui tant est digne de memoire, / Que ses euvres sont appellees / 'Miroir des dames mariees,' / Que j'ay emprises a rigmer / Afin que l'en s'i puist mirer / Et que pregnent en passience / Celles a qui vient pestillence" (vv. 7–14). Cf. *Erec*, vv. 9–22; Alexandre Micha, ed., *Les Romans de Chrétien de Troyes*, vol. 2: *Cligés*, CFMA, no. 84 (Paris: H. Champion, 1968), vv. 22–24; Mario Roques, ed., *Les Romans de Chrétien de Troyes*, vol. 4: *Le Chevalier au lion (Yvain)*, CFMA, no. 89 (Paris: H. Champion, 1965), vv. 33–41; William Roach, ed., *Le Roman de Perceval, ou Le Conte du Graal*,

2d ed., Textes Littéraires Français, no. 71 (Geneva: Droz, 1959), vv. 61–68.

13. Vv. 8, 45–46. Cf. *Erec*, vv. 23–24; *Cligés*, vv. 2345–46; Jean Renart, *L'Escoufle, roman d'aventure*, ed. Henri Michelant and Paul Meyer, Société des Anciens Textes Français [SATF] (Paris: Firmin Didot, 1894), vv. 27–37.

14. Henri de Ferrières, *Les Livres du roy Modus et de la royne Ratio*, ed. Gunnar Tilander, SATF, no. 73 (Paris: Firmin Didot, 1932).

15. Ibid., chaps. 117 and 118. See also Marcelle Thiébaux, "The Mediaeval Chase," *Speculum* 42 (1967): 263.

16. See my "The Hunting Scenes in *L'Estoire de Griseldis*," in *Voices of Conscience: Studies in Memory of James D. Powell and Rosemary Hodgins*, ed. Raymond J. Cormier (Philadelphia: Temple University Press, 1977), pp. 78–94.

17. Cf. *Erec et Enide*, vv. 2455–573; *Yvain*, vv. 2486–540; see also Edmund Reiss, "The Hero as Warrior and Lover: An Approach to the Theme of Chrétien's *Erec* and *Yvain*," *Bulletin Bibliographique de la Société Internationale Arthurienne* 15 (1963): 144.

18. Many passages are devoted to the reactions of the members of court: especially the comments of knights and barons regarding Gautier's indifference to marriage (vv. 156–269); the discussion between the Quint Chevalier and the Tiers Chevalier concerning Gautier's sudden choice of a bride (vv. 804–33); and the remarks of two ladies on the noble manners of Griseldis (vv. 1071–84) and on her countenance during the two years she has been without her daughter (vv. 1501–26). Frequently the courtiers praise Griseldis (vv. 1236–58; 2372–83) and underline the seemingly deviant behavior of the marquis (vv. 1801–52). These reactions offset the marquis's false and negative representations of the court when he addresses himself to Griseldis (vv. 1335–71; 1602–38; 2067–93).

19. Cf. vv. 1091–235, 2548–608. The shepherds are reminiscent of those in the *pastourelles*, where there exists a normative opposition between the knight and shepherd; see Zink, pp. 25–

116, for a useful discussion of the genre. Cf. Craig, p. 9: "The criticism of courtly life put into the mouth of the 'premier berger' (1091–235), while it undoubtedly echoes the traditional attitude of shepherds in the pastourelles, nevertheless gains force in that it probably voices the author's own revolt against the worldly life of courtiers of the time." Given this bias, the author may likewise have used these scenes to prevent the spectator from interpreting Griseldis as an emblem of upward social mobility.

20. "Beneoït soit qui l'engendra, / Qu'envoïe est des cieulz ça jus / Pour le bien publique et salus" (vv. 1251–53). These lines may have been inspired by Dioneo's concluding statement in the *Decameron* (X.x): "What more can we say, except that divine spirits may sometimes descend from heaven, even to wretched hovels, just as in kingly palaces others may be born who are fitter to keep swine than to rule over men?" (trans. Frances Winwar [New York: Modern Library, 1955], pp. 658–59).

21. The first half of the play ends at v. 1304, the first "act" at v. 1235. For bipartite structure in romance, see my "Trois sur deux: Théories de bipartition et de tripartition des oeuvres de Chrétien," in the issue of *Oeuvres et Critiques* devoted to "La Réception critique de l'oeuvre de Chrétien de Troyes," ed. Raymond J. Cormier (forthcoming).

22. Cf. Frank, p. 156.

Scottish Transformations of Courtly Literature

William Dunbar and the Court of James IV

FLORENCE H. RIDLEY

nformation about James IV and his household derives primarily from the king's correspondence with almost every royal power in western Europe, from the listing of his expenditures in the public records of Scotland, the comments of Erasmus, who served as tutor to James's son, the young archbishop of Saint Andrews, and the eyewitness account of Don Pedro de Ayala, Spanish ambassador to Scotland from Ferdinand and Isabella.[1] These sources conjure up a picture of a court inhabited by learned men, by musicians, minstrels, dancers, and actors, presided over by a monarch interested in learning, in languages, history, theology, architecture, and alchemy, with a marked taste for music, magic, pageants, poetry, and philandering. James, it seems, was a generous, impetuous, mercurial man, given to alternating extremes of dalliance and devoutness.[2] For fifteen years or more William Dunbar was associated with this king and his court, and the nature of the role he played there in large part determined the nature of the poetry he wrote.

Information about Scotland's premier poet can be gleaned from scattered references in contemporary records, from his own poetry, and from that portion of "The Flyting of Dunbar and Kennedy" composed by Walter Kennedy.[3] Of course, evidence from this last source must be taken with a grain of salt. A verbal slug-fest in which opponents pelt each other with clods of abuse is not the best context in which to seek accurate biographical data, although to date, every editor of and almost every commentator upon Dunbar has done precisely that. Thus it is generally, but not universally, agreed that the poet was born after the great eclipse of 18 July 1460, not only because the date accords with references in the rolls of Saint Andrews University to a "Willelmus" Dunbar, but also because in their mucky battle of words Kennedy says of his opponent, "Thou was consavit in the grete eclips," then draws unflattering conclusions about the effect of the darkness of the moon upon Dunbar's moral character.[4] Kennedy also tells of Dunbar's travels in the guise (if not the actual role) of a holy man, through Scotland then abroad, through France, and as far south as the foot of the Alps, then north again through Paris, perhaps even up into Denmark (ll. 355–56, 368, 425–38). The poet did become a peripatetic ecclesiastic, apparently a friar, for he tells us how "in freiris weid" he fawned, preached, and taught in "Dertoun kirk," "Canterberry," and "Piccardy."[5] But before August 1500 he returned from such wanderings to Edinburgh and joined the retinue of the king, who later made an offering when Master William Dunbar celebrated his first mass on 15 March 1504.[6]

The nature of the poet's role at court is not entirely clear. There is no evidence for Oliphant Smeaton's old theory that Bishop Robert Blackadder placed him "among the royal attendants" in order to "exercise a restraining influence on the youthful ruler's headstrong sensuality" and that Dunbar became "the monarch's confidential agent," performing "many delicate missions . . . of an amatory as well as of a political character."[7] Yet certain poems suggest that he may indeed at times have played Falstaff to a Scottish Prince Hal. The poet was, after all, only thirteen years older than James, and he celebrates, perhaps entered into, revels at court: dances, pageants, plays, tournaments. He mimics the baby talk of below-stairs seduction, jokes about courtiers smitten with the "pokkis," teases the king when he gets caught trying to seduce a village maid—the white lamb, hotly pursued by a red-bearded fox—and even dares to laugh at his penance in a parody of the Litany of the Dead which bids the king return from fasting in Stirling to feasting in Edinburgh.[8]

But if James was a philanderer, he was also a deeply religious man; and if Dunbar was a fellow reveler, he was also a priest. That role is suggested by other poems of his. "The Thrissil and the Rois" soberly admonishes the king to be faithful to his young bride, Margaret Tudor, the "fresche Rois, of collour reid and quhyt." The satires, "None May Assure in the World," "Remonstrance to the King," "A General Satyre," are scathing attacks upon the hypocrisy and injustice rampant at court. The moralizings, "All Erdly Joy Returnis in Pane," "Of Manis Mortalitie," "Of the Warldis Vanitie," are admonitions of a good pastor. The religious poems, on the Nativity, the Passion, the Resurrection, the manner of confession, are not only celebrations of the radiant beauty of worship but exhortations to devotion.

Although he is not designated "poet laureate" in any of the contemporary references that have survived, Dunbar is called "laureate" by Walter Kennedy; and the title seems an accurate definition of a role he played at court, that of an eminent poet who receives a stipend as an officer of the royal household, his duty being to write court-odes and other occasional verse. Certainly Dunbar was eminent. Gawin Douglas places him in the court of the muses in company with Chaucer, Gower, and Lydgate; and six, possibly seven, of his poems were among the first ever to be printed in Scotland.[9] From 15 August 1500, until 14 May 1513, in the disastrous year of Flodden which ended James's life, Dunbar received royal stipends, a steadily increasing pension, special bequests, and on two occasions money to pay for the gown he wanted "at yule."[10] He wrote odes to Aberdeen and to the great lord Bernard Stewart, poems for state occasions, such as the funeral of that same lord or the celebration of James's marriage, and poems that may be called "courtly" in every sense of that amorphous term. "Of, pertaining to, or connected with the Court," as witness the numerous addresses to the king or queen and accounts of court activities. "Having the state, elegance or refinement befitting a court," as witness the richly encrusted aureate allegories, "Bewty and the Presoneir," "The Thrissil and the Rois," "The Goldyn Targe," "The Merle and the Nychtingaill." "Appropriate to courts of law," as witness the legal phraseology in which the "Lady Solistaris" ply their trade at court.[11]

He even wrote verse that is "courtly" in the now archaic sense of "characterized by the fair words or flattery of courtiers,"[12] for Dunbar himself is occasionally guilty of flattery, the very vice he so often attacks. However, in all fairness, it should be acknowledged that the most glaring example of this particular vice is in a poem of doubtful authorship. If the portraits of Margaret Tudor as bride and as widow are true likenesses, she could scarcely ever have been what she is called in "To the Princess Margaret," the "fair, fairest of every fair, Princess most pleasant and pre-clare." But happily the poem is not always attributed to William Dunbar.[13]

References in Kennedy's portion of "The Flyting" as well as in Dunbar's own poetry to Germany, Holland, Picardy, France, Italy, and Spain indicate that he traveled widely and perhaps sojourned for a time in Europe. Such experience may account for the obvious continental influence upon his lyrics.[14] Whatever the cause, as James Kinsley says, Dunbar's "poetic inheritance was the courtly tradition of medieval France and England";[15] and in his role of poet laureate he wrote many perfectly conventional courtly poems. He also wrote poems that make a most unconventional use of courtly genres and themes, rhythms and rimes—the ballade, *chanson d'aventure*, complaint, *demande d'amour*, dream vision, poetic testament, celebration of knightly prowess, stanzaic patterns reminiscent of romance and the lyrics of Provence and Burgundy—to produce irony. Thus "The Tua Mariit Wemen and the Wedo" begins as a conventional *chanson d'aventure*. The poet walks out on Midsummer Eve to a green garden where he spies three ladies royally arrayed, their glittering hair garlanded with fresh flowers, their faces meek, white, fair as sweet lilies or the new blown rose; and attracted by their "hie speiche" and "hautand [haughty] wourdis" he

listens to their "many sundry tailes." But with the opening gambit of the widow, "Bewrie . . . ye woddit women
ying, / Quhat mirth ye fand in maryage, sen ye war menis
wyffis" (ll. 41–42), the poet and the reader are catapulted
into a rollicking *chanson de mal mariée*, as the high speech of
the ladies plummets to the level of fishwives, with words
that, as Henry Higgins so aptly put it, would make a sailor
blush. Quoth one:

> I have ane wallidrag, ane worme, ane auld wobat carle,
> A waistit wolroun, na worth bot wourdis to clatter;
> Ane bumbart, ane dron bee, ane bag full of flewme,
> Ane skabbit skarth, ane scorpioun, ane scutarde behind;
> To see him scart his awin skyn grit scunner I think.
> Quhen kissis me that carybald, than kyndillis all my sorow;
> As birs of ane brym bair, his berd is als stif,
> Bot soft and soupill as the silk is his sary lume;
> He may weill to the syn assent, bot sakles is his deidis.★
>   [ll. 89–97]

Thus the poet uses the courtly high style as a medium of
coarse, erotic reminiscence, and the ludicrous inappropri-
ateness of such memories and language from such persons
in such a setting makes the poem a burlesque. In the context of this gleeful lashing of their hapless husbands by

★I have a sloven, a worm, an old caterpillar carl,
  A wasted mongrel, no worth but words to clatter;
  A drone, a drone bee, a bag full of phlegm,
  A scabby cormorant, a scorpion, an evacuator behind;
  To see him scratch his own skin great disgust I think.
  When kisses me that monster, then kindles all my sorrow;
  As bristles of a fierce boar, his beard is as stiff,
  But soft and supple is his sorry tool;
  He may well to the sin assent, but innocent are his deeds.

these "ladies," the *demande d'amour* with which the poem ends has brought laughter, and perhaps a shudder, for four hundred years:

> Ye auditoris most honorable, that eris has gevin
> Oneto this uncouth aventur, quhilk airly me happinnit;
> Of thir thre wantoun wiffis, that I haif writtin heir,
> Quhilk wald ye waill to your wif, gif ye suld wed one? †
>
> [ll. 527–30]

This technique, I believe, results in Dunbar's most striking transformations of courtly literature.

We find it everywhere. In "Of Sir Thomas Norny" and "The Sowtar and Tailyouris War," where with the *rime couée* of romance Dunbar depicts the antics of the king's fool and the knightly jousting of a rabble of cobblers and tailors. In "Of Ane Blak-Moir," where a royal tournament is held for the dubious prize of kissing a slave's backside. In dream visions that deal not with the conventional lover's quest but with the lurid dance of the seven deadly sins or the abortive flight of a feigned friar covered with stuck-on chicken feathers. In a courtly lyric, a variant of the Burgundian *complainte amoureuse*,[16] which rather than praising, condemns love for its inconstancy:

> Quha will behald of luve the chance,
> With sueit dissavyng countenance,
> In quhais fair dissimulance
> May none assure; . . .

---

† Ye listeners most honorable, that ears have given
   To this strange adventure, which happened to me early,
   Of these three wanton wives, that I have written here,
   Which would ye choose for your wife, if ye should wed one?

> In luve to keip allegance,
> It war als nys an ordinance,
> As quha wald bid ane deid man dance
>   In sepulture.[17]

And in another written, "Quhone he List to Feyne":

> My hartis tresure, and swete assured fo,
>   The finale endar of my lyfe for ever;
> The creuell brekar of my hart in tuo,
>   To go to deathe, this I deservit never;
>   O man slayer! quhill saule and life dissever
> Stynt of your slauchter; Allace! your man am I,
> A thousand tymes that dois yow mercy cry.
>
> . . . .
>
> In to my mynd I sall yow mercye cry,
>   Quhone that my toung sall faill me to speik,   [when
> And quhill that nature me my sycht deny,   [until
>   And quhill my ene for pane incluse and steik,
>   [eyes, shut, shut
>   And quhill the dethe my hart in sowndir breik,
>   And quhill my mynd may think and towng may steir;
> And syne, fair weill, my hartis Ladie deir!   [then
>   [ll. 1–7, 43–49]

That twist in the concluding couplet turns the poem into something directly opposed to what its courtly terminology and *chant royal* stanza have led us to expect. It is reminiscent of Chaucer and anticipatory of Shakespeare.

"The Ladyis Solistaris at Court" is "courtly" in almost every sense of the word: "of the king's court," for it is an attack on the corrupt practices of James's courtiers and their wives; "of the law courts," for it is couched throughout in legal metaphors; "elegant, refined," for the poem's ostensible theme is praise of fair ladies, and its tripping movement is that of a minuet;

Thir ladyis fair, That makis repair
And in the court ar kend,   [known
Thre dayis thair Thay will do mair
Ane matter for till end,
Than thair gud men Will do in ten,
For any craft thay can,
So weill thay ken Quhat tyme and quhen [know, What, when
Thair menes thay sowld mak than.   [complaints

With littill noy Thay can convoy   [annoyance, conduct
Ane matter fynaly,
Richt myld and moy, And keip it coy,   [demure
On evyns quyetly.
Thay do no mis, Bot gif thay kis,
And keipis collatioun,   [refreshment before bed
Quhat rek of this? Thair matter is
Brocht to conclusion. . . .

Thairfoir I reid, Gif ye haif pleid,   [debate in law court
Or matter in to pley,   [to place in litigation
To mak remeid, Send in your steid   [remedy
Your ladeis grathit up gay.   [dressed
Thay can defend Evin to the end
Ane matter furth expres;
Suppois thay spend, It is unkend,   [unknown
Thair geir is nocht the les.   [goods
In quyet place, Thocht thay haid space
Within les nor twa howris,   [less than
Thay can, percaice, Purches sum grace   [perhaps
At the compositouris.   [settler of disputes
Thair compositioun, With full remissioun,
                                    [agreement, forgiveness
Thair fynaly is endit,
With expeditioun And full conditioun   [points in a compact
And thairto seilis appendit.

It is a light, dancing thing, and a deadly satire. The complex, French-type quatrain, with its double internal rime

repeated four times, produces a delicacy and an airy grace that intensify the irony, because the courtly sound and movement are admirably suited for woman as the epitome of elegance and honor; yet they serve to tell of her gross corruption. These "ladyis fair" are selling their bodies so that their pimp husbands can gain favors at court. "Solisters" they are; "ladies" they are not.

A number of critics have remarked upon the versatility of this Scottish poet, most notably perhaps John Leyerle in his "The Two Voices of William Dunbar."[18] Poet laureate, priest, companion of the king, he wrote admirable poems to serve every turn at the court of James IV. But to my mind in those transformations of courtly conventions wherein he made a yoking of dissimilarities, of "hautand" manner with realistic matter, he created humor and irony that had been unmatched in the British Isles since the rondel of "Merciles Beautee" and was not to be matched again until the sonnet "My Mistress' Eyes Are Nothing Like the Sun."

NOTES

1. *The Letters of James the Fourth, 1505–1513*, calendared by Robert Kerr Hannay, ed. R. L. Mackie, Publications of the Scottish History Society, series 3, vol. 45 (Edinburgh, 1953); *Compota Thesauriorum regum Scotorum, Accounts of the Lord High Treasurer of Scotland*, vol. 1, ed. Thomas Dickson, vols. 2–6, ed. James Balfour Paul (Edinburgh: H.M. General Register House, 1877–1902); *Registrum magni sigilli regum Scotorum, The Register of the Great Seal of Scotland*, vol. 2, ed. James Balfour Paul (Edinburgh: H.M. General Register House, 1882); *Rotuli*

Saccarium regum Scotorum, The Exchequer Rolls of Scotland, vols. 9–12, ed. G. Burnett, vol. 13, ed. G. Burnett and AE. J. G. Mackay (Edinburgh: H.M. General Register House, 1886–91); *Registrum secreti sigilli regum Scotorum, The Register of the Privy Seal of Scotland*, vol. 1, ed. M. Livingstone (Edinburgh: H.M. General Register House, 1908); Pedro de Ayala, in *Calendar of Letters, Despatches and State Papers Relating to the Negotiations between England and Spain*, ed. G. A. Bergenroth (London: Longman, Green, Longman and Roberts, 1862), no. 210; D. Erasmus, *Adagiorum Chiliades* ii.v.1, in *Opera omnia*, ed. J. Leclerc (Leiden: P. Vander Aa, 1703), vol. 2, p. 544. For discussion and summary of other sources of information cf. G. Gregory Smith, ed., *The Days of James iiij, 1488–1513* (London: D. Nutt, 1900), and R. L. Mackie, *King James IV of Scotland* (Edinburgh: Oliver and Boyd, 1958).

2. For James's illicit affairs as well as his regular attendance at religious observances, see "Daily Life" in Mackie, *King James IV*.

3. *Acta Facultatis Artium S. Andreae*, Saint Andrews University, pp. 76, 79; *Accounts of the Lord High Treasurer of Scotland*, vol. 1, passim; *The Register of the Privy Seal of Scotland*, vol. 1, passim. Most of the references in the public records are reproduced by AE. J. G. Mackay in "Appendix to Introduction," *The Poems of William Dunbar*, ed. John Small, Publications of the Scottish Text Society [PSTS], 16 (Edinburgh and London: Scottish Text Society, 1889), pp. cliii–clvi. "Flyting" is poetical invective, chiefly a kind of contest in which two persons assail each other alternately with tirades of abuse, cf. *OED*: 'Fliting, flyting,' 1.+b. The practice of verbal combat was a very old, widespread one going back to Ovid and found among the French, Italian, Anglo-Saxon, and Celtic writers. For "The Flyting of Dunbar and Kennedie," see *The Poems of William Dunbar*, ed. W. Mackay Mackenzie (1932; rpt. London: John Dickens, 1970); all quotations of Dunbar's poetry are from this edition. For discussion of the improbable biographical significance of the

poem, "How Dumbar wes Desyrd to be Ane Freir," cf. A. G. Rigg, "William Dunbar: The 'Fenyeit Freir,'" *Review of English Studies*, n.s. 15 (1963): 269–73.

4. Cf. *Acta Facultatis Artium S. Andreae*: J. W. Baxter, *William Dunbar: A Biographical Study* (Edinburgh: Oliver and Boyd, 1952), pp. 9–10; and "The Flyting," lines 489 and passim. Among others who have cited the passage in "The Flyting" in substantiation of the date of Dunbar's birth are Baxter, p. 10; Mackenzie, p. xix; and Mackie, *King James IV*, p. 175. For a brief survey of previous opinions regarding the date of the poet's birth and advocacy of a different eclipse as the proper starting point for its calculation, cf. Denton Fox, "The Chronology of William Dunbar," *Philological Quarterly* 39 (1960), particularly pp. 413–15.

5. "How Dumbar wes Desyrd to be Ane Freir," ll. 36–40. Mackie, *King James IV*, pp. 175–76, taking this particular poem at face value, sees Dunbar as a Scottish Villon, a vagabond scholar who wore the garb of Saint Francis only as a "disguise." Admittedly the evidence is ambiguous, since Dunbar depicts himself as rejecting the invitation of Saint Francis, actually the devil in disguise. But James IV was a vigorous supporter of the Franciscan order (cf. *The Letters*, pp. 55–56), and I would suggest that this poem is a spoof, comparable to "The Dregy of Dunbar," a goliardic parody of the Litany of the Dead, or to the parodies that Mackie, p. 121, says were roared out at court by choristers on Saint Nicholas's Day. Dunbar was just as capable of being a genuine Franciscan friar and satirizing the order as he was of being a genuine priest and writing parodies of the worship service.

6. *Accounts of the Lord High Treasurer* records payments to him from 1501 until 14 May 1513, as well as the king's offering on the occasion of his first mass. *The Privy Seal Register*, vol. 2, f. 9, records a gift of £10 made on 15 August 1500.

7. Oliphant Smeaton, *William Dunbar* (New York: Charles Scribner's Sons, 1898), pp. 46–51. The fiction was picked up

and elaborated upon by Clement Armstrong in "William Dunbar and His Times," *Transactions of the Hawick Archaeological Society*, 12th meeting, 17 November 1908 (Hawick, 1908), pp. 86–94; Violet Jacob, in "James IV and His Poet," *The Scots Magazine* 10 (1929): 276–82; and Mackay, *King James IV*, p. xxx.

8. See those poems listed by Mackenzie under the heading "Court Life."

9. "The Palice of Honour," ll. 918–24, in *The Shorter Poems of Gavin Douglas*, ed. Priscilla J. Bawcutt, PSTS, 4th series, no. 3 (East Lothian: Scottish Text Society; London: Blackwood, 1967), 3:62–63. MS National Library of Scotland 19 1 16, *Porteous of Noblenes and Ten Other Rare Tracts* (Edinburgh: W. Chepman and A. Myllar, 1508), pp. 88–100, 137–44, 169–74, 177–96 (see Baxter, p. 178, for comment).

10. These payments are listed in *The Privy Seal Register* and *The Accounts of the Lord High Treasurer* and reproduced by Mackay, pp. cliii–clvi.

11. *OED*: "courtly," *a*. 1, 3. *A Dictionary of the Older Scottish Tongue*, ed. William A. Craigie (Chicago: University of Chicago Press, 1937), 1:715: "Courtly, -lie," *a*. 1, and especially 2. "Appropriate to courts of law."

12. *OED*: "courtly," *a*, 4.

13. See the portraits of Margaret Tudor reproduced by Mackie, *King James IV*, and by John Small in *The Poetical Works of Gavin Douglas*, vol. 1 (1874; rpt., Hildesheim, N.Y.: G. Olms, 1970). The poem is not accepted as Dunbar's by Mackenzie.

14. See particularly "The Flyting," ll. 355, 368, 380, 433–38, and "How Dumbar was Desyrd to be Ane Freir." For discussions of the French influence upon Dunbar's poetry, cf. Tom Scott, in *Dunbar, a Critical Exposition of the Poems* (Edinburgh and London: Oliver and Boyd, 1966), pp. 307, 310–31; and Janet M. Smith, *The French Background of Middle Scots Literature* (Edinburgh and London: Oliver and Boyd, 1934), passim.

15. In the introduction to *William Dunbar, Poems* (Oxford: Clarendon Press, 1958), p. xi.

16. Cf. Molinet no. 17. The form of the *complainte amoureuse* was said to have been invented by Arnoul Greban.

17. "Inconstancy of Luve," ll. 1–4, 21–24. The poem must be read in its entirety for any real appreciation of the consummate skill with which Dunbar adapts Middle Scots to the strict lyric measure.

18. *University of Toronto Quarterly* 31 (1962): 316–38.

A Courtly Paradox
in Book VI of Spenser's *Faerie Queene*

WINIFRED GLEESON KEANEY

One of the paradoxes of courtly love is the equivocal function of woman in that scheme of ritualized devotion which, articulated in diction drawn from religion and feudalism, offers worship and service to the lady. Simultaneously, however, her elevated status is placed in jeopardy by the loyalties defined in religious and feudal tradition. In both, man owes his allegiance to his lord, and in both, the entrance of a woman renders the bond of loyalty a bulky triangular tension. Woman becomes a distraction, and however she may be asserted as ennobling, she carries the pejorative connotations of Eve and Delilah, always threatening to undermine man's spiritual and martial prowess.[1]

This tension is incongruous in courtly love—especially when we conceive of that love as crucial in the code of courtly behavior. The impression a man makes upon a woman he loves is one way of defining himself. Mastering the rituals of this love confers an aristocratic status, yet it also brings out the duality of his nature, which both inclines to enjoy and professes to transcend worldly delights.

A moral paradox seems to underlie the social one, in that the ennobling power of this love derives in part from its adulterous character. E. Talbot Donaldson has remarked

that "those scholars who place most emphasis on a supposed cult of adultery are often the ones who, like Lewis,
are most anxious to moralize the Middle Ages."[2] In definitions of courtly love there is much equivocation about the
physical; from the "pure love" of the troubadours of
southern France, it seems only a short step to "mixed
love," which includes physical gratification. The problem
is that modern historians cannot be sure when and how
often that step was taken.[3]

For the troubadours, pure love was a union of the hearts
and minds of the lovers, desire and yearning for one's lady,
productive of joy, and ennobling to the lover. This love
could include a desire for the sensuous and encouraged all
that could provoke such desire in a physically unconsum-
mated affair. Such was courtly love, and it was preferable
to, though not exclusive of, mixed love—which would
begin pure but terminate in physical union. Mixed love,
considered inferior to the pure because it was often transient and was likely to minimize, if not end, desire, was also
real love, since it proceeded from the same concupiscible
feeling of the heart and had as its substance desire. The
morality of courtly love was determined thus: "Does love
further a man in virtue or does it effect a regress; does it
ennoble him or degrade him?"[4] In this conception, it was
desire that ennobled.

The claims for the power of love to render man more
noble are also evident in the tales of chivalry. A knight will
challenge another both seriously and arbitrarily in order to
protect and impress his lady. There is enough variety and
ambiguity in medieval literary representations of courtly

love so that we can point to examples where love ennobles the male lover, as well as others where it vitiates his progress toward his ultimate goals. More often man compromises, trading some public shame for victory in love (Lancelot dishonors himself by mounting the cart, yet he moves on through chivalric feats to merit the love of Guinevere).

The writers of the English Renaissance, influenced by the Italians, wrestle with the place of the woman. Often they profess to define her as a heavenly inspiration, a stimulus to a transcendent experience,[5] but still they incorporate the negatives traditionally associated with femininity.[6] For instance, in Elizabethan sonnets, there is the paradoxical situation of the poet pursuing the lady who makes him suffer. From Spenser's *Amoretti*:

> And happy lines, on which with starry light,
> Those lamping eyes will deigne sometimes to look
> And reade the sorrows of my dying spright,
> Written with teares in harts close bleeding book
> [I.5–8]

> Till then I wander careful comfortlesse,
> In secret sorrow and sad pensivenesse.
> [XXXIV.13–14]

> Yet she, beholding me with constant eye,
> Delights not in my merth nor rues my smart:
> But when I laugh she mocks, and when I cry
> She laughs and hardens evermore her heart.
> [LIV.9–12][7]

In *Astrophel and Stella* Sidney understands that his love for Stella is contrary to his best thinking and reason:

> True, that on earth we are but pilgrims made,
> And should in soul up to our country move.
> True, and yet true that I must Stella love.
>
>   [v.12–14]
>
> Reason, in faith thou art well served, that still
> Wouldst brabbling be with sense and love in me;
>
>   [x.1–2]

Yet Stella apparently does not reward his sacrifice; he asks the moon:

> Are beauties there as proud as here they be?
> Do they above love to be loved, and yet
> Those lovers scorn whom that love doth possess?
> Do they call virtue there ungratefulness?
>
>   [xxxi.11–14][8]

In Shakespeare's plays it becomes clear, on occasion, that love for a woman can thwart man's nobler accomplishments. Othello vows defensively that his love for Desdemona will not minimize his martial prowess;[9] friendship between two men is tested against the love of a man for a woman in *The Merchant of Venice*. Man's role, his goal, his "manliness" is still measured, and often jeopardized, by the manner in which he treats his lady. Renaissance man's concern with his proper place in the world is not free from the influence of his medieval ancestors; the old ideal of courtly behavior was still personally and publicly valued. And the function of the lady in that code remains crucial, though still ambivalent.

I will discuss this ambivalence in one of the Renaissance "courtesy books," Book VI of Spenser's *Faerie Queene*. Spenser's poem is in the tradition of Renaissance humanism; it specifies the qualities that constitute a gentleman, and it patterns a function for that man in the world. Both the private and public aspects of courtesy are important to Sir Calidore and his companions in Book VI. While the virtue of each book is conspicuous in *The Faerie Queene*, the emphasis seems to be on the individual's search to attain it. There are few perfect figures in Spenser's world; his knights err often, but they learn from their mistakes and come closer to virtue through experience. The episodic structure of romance and the labyrinthine forest settings allow for multiple examples of education by trial and error. The chivalric tradition provides the quest and the expectation of courtly behavior toward women. The knights test their dignity and worth according to this tradition. Especially in Spenser's work, we expect that the loyalties to duty and love will not conflict. We assume that knights will be ennobled by their love and esteem for women, for Spenser gives prominence and intelligence to women, and he resolves the spiritual/physical (or "pure" and "mixed") dilemma in the compromise of married love. Throughout he ascribes his motives and poetic competence to Gloriana (Elizabeth). In Book I Una cautions and corrects the Redcrosse Knight. Britomart, in Books III, IV, and V, is a lady knight of power and grace. In Book III Venus and Diana come to agreement, modifying the traditional dichotomy between the sensuous and the pure; and in Book VI the female is central to the action of almost every episode.[10] Yet in spite of all his professions to the contrary, Spenser incorporates the other half of the paradox into his work. In Book VI, the Book of Courtesy, woman is potentially destructive.[11] She has elegance and beauty, but she is a distraction from the business of the quest and is often full of enticement, guile, and deception. Man is less than manly when he devotes his attention to woman. Her very assets are his weakness, and the quandary that he thus faces is a curious aspect of his search to define himself.

In Spenser's Book of Courtesy, Sir Calidore's quest is to subdue the Blatant Beast, a symbol of social disharmony.[12] Many critics agree that courtesy is here a moral, social virtue, concerned with behavior toward others. Kathleen Williams describes it as "a delicate concern for others," one which has "much to do with nature, providence, love, death, and the generous exchanges of compassion and mutual respect among men." C. S. Lewis tells us that "we are to conceive of courtesy as the poetry of conduct." Humphrey Tonkin defines it as a moral quality, one which springs from a sense of responsibility to others, and Dorothy Woodward Culp as a virtue governing relationships with others, a basic duty to help others. In this sense, man attains true courtesy by behaving responsibly toward his fellow human beings. More particularly, it is noted often that Calidore learns what true courtesy is and thus attains it by means of his pastoral sojourn and his rescue of Pastorella from the Brigands.[13] Thus courtesy is defined in Book VI in a social way. Man can embody the virtue in his conduct toward others, and especially, he merits the descriptive epithet courteous in Book VI because of his chivalric activity in behalf of the woman.

It is appropriate that Book VI be so filled with women, for Spenser locates the pattern for the "praise of princely Curtesie" in Elizabeth:

> But where shall I in all antiquity
> So faire a pattern find, where may be seene
> The goodly praise of princely Curtesie,
> As in yourself, O soveraine Lady Queene [14]
>   [Intro. 6]

The praise emanates from her mind, reflecting as a mirror does and inflaming with brightness all who look on her. It is possible that the ambiguity of Spenser's phrasing makes the queen a model of appreciation of courtesy rather than a model of courtesy. In the former sense she can be an inspiration for courteous behavior and one who can acknowledge and affirm courteous behavior. Certainly she is (as are all the women in Book VI) capable of acting either courteously or discourteously, but I suggest that the emphasis here is on courtesy as essentially manly, and on women as both prompting and thwarting the achievement of courteous action.

In general Calidore's "manliness" or his proof of his own worth depends on the fulfillment of his quest; he should also behave gently and courteously on his mission, as befits a knight in the service of Gloriana, the Faerie Queene. Among the qualifications for such behavior, as Calidore sees it, is service to women:

> For knights and all men this by nature have,
> Towards all womenkind them kindly to behave.
>   [ii. 14]

Calidore lives by his own dictum; in the course of his quest, he protects, rescues, or yields to the pleas of the damsel pursued by Maleffort, Briana, Priscilla, Serena, and Pastorella. Calepine does the same for Serena and

Matilde; Arthur for Mirabella and Blandina; Tristram for the dead knight's lady and for Priscilla; the salvage man for Serena; and Timias attempts the rescue of Serena and Mirabella.

That women need the protection of knights is evident; it is also clear that they inspire and affirm courteous behavior. Women provide innumerable opportunities for men to overextend themselves, thereby proving their knightly worth and prowess. The damsels in distress serve another function: if courtesy can be quantified, the measure is discernible in the rescue episodes. Turpine denies hospitality to the wounded Serena and later proves himself not only discourteous but also a sniveling coward. Calepine is a less effective protector of Serena than are Calidore and the salvage man. Calidore outclasses Coridon to win first Pastorella's love and then her gratitude. Arthur intercedes to remedy Timias's abortive attempts to rescue Serena and Mirabella. Service to women ennobles men, and it also allows us to determine which man is more noble than another.

The women of Book VI are comely and fair, and Spenser praises them often. In canto x, Colin Clout explains to Calidore the idyllic scene that vanished when the latter showed himself. The dancing ladies were Venus's damsels, the Graces, daughters of Jove and Eurynome. It is these graces, Colin tells Calidore, figured as women, from whom men derive all that is courteous:

> "These three on men all gracious gifts bestow,
> Which decke the body or adorne the mynde,
> To make them lovely or well favoured show,
> As comely carriage, entertainement kynde

> Sweet semblaunt, friendly offices that bynde,
> And all the complements of curtesie:
> They teach us, how to each degree and kynde
> We should our selves demeane, to low, to hie,
> To friends, to foes; which skill men call civility."
>
> [x.23]

In a more practical way Spenser affirms the power women hold over men. At the beginning of canto viii there is an admonition to "gentle ladies," claiming that Love has left the glory of his kingdom and the hearts of men to them as their dowry. Both the glory and the hearts are bound to women "in yron chaines, of liberty bereft," a gift delivered into the hands of women. Women are warned against the tyranny of pride and cautioned to be "soft and tender eeke in mynde," to chase cruelty and hardness from their natures. The reverse example is Mirabella's case, which has been tried in Cupid's court and which is exemplary of discourteous behavior. Mirabella's crime is that she was beautiful and much admired and did not deem those who loved her worthy of her love; thus she lost twenty-two lovers. The reciprocity between admiration and the meriting of admiration is evident in Spenser's description of Mirabella's status:

> Unworthy she to be belov'd so dere,
> That could not weight of worthinesse aright:
> For beautie is more glorious bright and clere,
> The more it is admir'd of many a wight
> And noblest she that served is of noblest knight.
>
> [vii.29]

The circle seems to grow tighter; just as men's hearts are bound in chains to women, women are not free not to love men. A knight gains in nobility by virtue of his love for a woman, and the act of such loving confers nobility on that woman. It is interesting that Pastorella seems guilty of precisely the same crime when Calidore first meets her, yet she is not described as disdainful and scornful (as was Mirabella), nor is she tried and convicted:

> Ne was there heard, ne was there shepheards swayne,
> But did her honour, and eke many a one
> Burnt in her love, and with sweet pleasing payne
> Full many a night for her did sigh and grone:
> But most of all the shepheard Coridon
> For her did languish, and his deare life spend;
> Yet neither she for him nor other none
> Did care a whit, ne any liking lend:
> Though meane her lot, yet higher did her mind ascend
>   [ix.10]

Both of these women hold dominion over men's hearts, and though it becomes clear that Pastorella was waiting for the most courteous man, Calidore, it also seems fair to wonder if Mirabella was not also waiting for an ideal man and if she does not deserve the same respect given to Pastorella. The point, however, is that women hold power and that the consequences of that power can be both disastrous and ennobling.

There are other instances of women's destructiveness in Book VI. Men are creatures of the flesh, and occasionally Spenser allows them to evidence a simple, uncomplicated lust: the knight whom Tristram has killed deserved his fate because he attacked Aladine only in order to enjoy the pleasures of Aladine's lady Priscilla, although he was accompanied by a lady of his own. When the members of the salvage nation come upon the sleeping Serena, they relish the meal that she will constitute for them. But when she awakes, their gourmandizing is superseded by sexual temptations. Her naked body in motion evokes their lascivious inclinations, and their physical consummation is restrained not by courtesy but by religion (she has been promised as a sacrifice to the gods).

Although man is susceptible to the physical temptations, the consequences of attraction to a lady are usually more subtle; often, his right judgment is impaired because he has been taken over by the lady's charm. Evil is not always apparent; an example of a deceptively appealing façade is Blandina. As the lady of the uncivil, cowardly Turpine, she seems relatively gentle and merciful. She reproves Turpine's rudeness to Calepine's original salute (iii.32), entreats him to grant Calepine and Serena lodging (iii.42), and wins mercy for him from Arthur with her prayers and vows (vi.31). After he has subdued Turpine, Arthur upbraids him for his crimes against courtesy and condemns him for his faintness and cowardice. In the course of this denunciation Arthur sets up an opposition:

> Yet doest thou not with manhood, but with guile
> Maintaine this evill use, thy foes thereby to foile.
>
> [vi.34]

Directly contrary to manhood is guile, and Turpine, who has reneged on the one in favor of the other, is berated at length. Having promised Turpine's life to Blandina, Arthur goes back to the hall to find his companion, the salvage man. They return to the chamber of Blandina and Turpine to enjoy an evening's entertainment, but the salvage man, sighting Turpine, breaks into a rage and would destroy the knight except for Arthur's intervention.

In his comments on the evening's entertainment, Spenser makes his point: Arthur, who knows that guile is despicable, does not know guile when he sees it. The salvage man's instincts were right, and Arthur was wrong to yield to Blandina's pleas. For Blandina is false:

> For well she knew the wayes to win good will
> Of every wight, that were not too infest,
> And how to please the minds of good and ill,
> Through tempering of her words and lookes by wondrous skill.
>
> [vi.41]
>
> Yet were her words and lookes but false and fayned,
> To some hind end to make more easie way,
>
> [vi.42]

She can fawn and flatter, smiling smoothly, cloaking her intent with an appropriate "Yet were her words but wynd, and all her teares but water" (vi.42).

For Spenser the real villain in this episode is Blandina, who is the more dangerous because she seems not to be so. There are two associations to be made here. The first can be drawn from that which qualifies Blandina as guileful: her facility to deceive and to effect wrong with her speech. In this she is much like the Blatant Beast, the foe of courtesy. The Beast is always characterized with reference to his multiple vile tongues (v.xii.41; vi.i.8–9; vi.xii.27–30), and the first thing Calidore does once he has subdued the Beast is to muzzle his mouth, thereby rendering him harmless. In one sense, Blandina is more a menace to courtesy than is the Blatant Beast, for everyone recognizes the obvious threat, but even the exemplary Arthur is deceived by the "pleasing tongue" of guile. The second association is drawn by Spenser himself; Blandina's insidiousness is not unique to her—rather it is a characteristic of her sex:

> Whether such grace were given her by kynd,
> As women wont their guileful wits to guyde,
> Or learn'd the art to please, I doe not fynd.
>
> [vii.43]

Whether naturally or by artifice, women ordinarily have "guileful wits," and thus if Blandina is analogous to the Blatant Beast, so are most women. Arthur has described "manhood" and "guile" as mutually exclusive modes of behavior. Spenser now establishes guile as a typically female trait. It seems evident that women can constitute a threat to manliness just as the Blatant Beast is a threat to courtesy.

Spenser establishes clearly the potential destructiveness of women; he also includes in this book evidence that man is more vulnerable when he is in love, and that the attainment of his chivalric quest is thereby jeopardized. This evidence weighs against the implicit assertion that love for a woman inspires a knight to greater achievement and glory. In spite of all the honor accrued in the service of damsels in distress, love and conquest, often love and honor, are at odds. Loyalty to a woman is not always congruous with loyalty to the quest. D. W. Robertson cites sources from classical and medieval writers which describe the contradictory nature of the warrior as lover: Ovid implies that physical love is inconsistent with military virtue; John of Salisbury explains that nothing is more contrary to knight-

hood than lechery; Walter of Châtillon claims that sexual
love debilitates those who hold positions of political power.[15] At times Spenser too seems to subscribe to the in-
compatibility of physical love with the achievement of
serious goals. Men put aside their armor to enjoy the com-
panionship of ladies, and repeatedly in Book VI they are
vulnerable to subsequent attack.

Spenser tells us of Aladine, sitting in "joyous jolliment"
with Priscilla:

> Unarm'd all was the knight, as then more meete,
> For ladies service and for loves delight.
>
> [ii.18]

The unprepared Aladine was set upon and left for dead by
an errant, lustful knight. Calepine too had divested himself
of his arms in order to "solace with his lady in delight."
Almost immediately the Blatant Beast rushed out of the
forest, snatched up Serena, and fled with her in his jaws.
Later, as Calepine walked beside the wounded Serena,
who rode on his horse, he was mocked and his manhood
was challenged as Turpine taunted him for being un-
horsed. Still later, when Calepine is lost, the salvage man
accompanies Serena in search of him. When something
goes amiss with Serena's horse, the salvage man puts Calepine's "combrous armes" aside in order to assist her. Almost at once Arthur and Timias ride up; Timias sees the
armor on the ground and precipitately battles with the
salvage man until Serena stops him. In the land of the shepherds, Calidore, having realized that Pastorella is not impressed by his knightly trappings, exchanges them for
shepherd's weeds in order to win her love. He seems to

have learned something that the others have not, though, for when he goes to the Brigands' cave to rescue her, he retains his shepherd's dress but arms himself "privily" underneath.

The most obvious illustration of the conflict of loyalties is Calidore's sojourn with the shepherds. Whether Spenser means us to disapprove of Calidore's truancy in this pastoral interlude or to understand it as a necessary educative process is open to debate.[16] What is certain is that Spenser points to Calidore's delinquency and labels it as such. Our first indication that love will conquer even Calidore comes early in this episode, when Calidore sights Pastorella, is smitten by her beauty, and

> So stood he still long gazing thereupon.
> Ne any will had thence to move away,
> Although his quest were farre afore him gon;
> [ix.7]

He is soon "rapt with double ravishment," enticed by the idyllic pastoral peace and the grace of Pastorella. What happens to Calidore here is perhaps, in microcosm, what makes love for a woman so threatening to man, for "He lost himselfe, and like one half entraunced grew" (ix.26).

Such a loss is lamentable, according to Spenser. He opens canto x with this question:

> Who now does follow the foule Blatant Beast,
> Whilest Calidore does follow that faire mayd,
> Unmyndfull of his vow, and high beheast
> Which by the Faery Queene was on him layd,
> That he should never leave, nor be delayd
> From chacing him, till he had it achieved?
> [x.1]

Spenser speaks of his knight as "entrapt" and "betrayd" by love, and he notes that the quest for the Beast has been replaced by the quest for Pastorella's love. Calidore has put aside his armor and has been wounded by an "envenimd sting," a "poysnous point deepe fixed in his hart." Eventually, Calidore will leave this world to resume his quest, but he does so when he has no alternative: the Brigands have spoiled the homes and killed the inhabitants of the pastoral world. Only Pastorella is left, and Calidore brings her back to civilization with him, where she finds her place.

Throughout Book VI Spenser shows us his knights as they strive for courtesy. The women in their lives inhibit courteous action as often as they inspire it. Man's attempts to define himself by his behavior toward women is often foiled when his manly identity is challenged by that behavior. The essential paradox of the medieval courtly notion of love plagues Renaissance man as effectively as it did his medieval ancestors.

NOTES

1. In the introduction to *Women as Image in Medieval Literature* (New York: Columbia University Press, 1975), Joan Ferrante discusses the religious and physiological theories of sex which helped to shape the pejorative connotation.

2. E. Talbot Donaldson, "The Myth of Courtly Love," in *Speaking of Chaucer* (New York: W. W. Norton, 1972), p. 162.

3. For discussions of this, see Joan M. Ferrante and George D. Economou, eds., *In Pursuit of Perfection: Courtly Love in Medieval Literature* (New York: Kennikat Press, 1975), pp. 3–15; Etienne Gilson, "St. Bernard and Courtly Love," appendix 4 of

The Mystical Theology of Saint Bernard (New York: Sheed and Ward, 1940; Douglas Kelly, "Courtly Love in Perspective: The Hierarchy of Love in Andreas Capellanus," *Traditio* 24 (1968): 119–41; Douglas Kelly, *Love and Marriage in the Age of Chaucer* (Ithaca: Cornell University Press, 1975).

4. Alexander T. Denomy, *The Heresy of Courtly Love* (Gloucester, Mass.: Peter Smith, 1965), p. 28.

5. Ferrante and Economou, pp. 11–13.

6. Gillian Beer examines (briefly) the use of romance in the Renaissance in *The Romance* (London: Metheun, 1970), pp. 17–38. More often, discussion of the detrimental effects of woman in the Renaissance occurs in examinations of the conflict in man between passion and reason, body and soul. Lily B. Campbell cites historical sources for these examinations in *Shakespeare's Tragic Heroes* (Cambridge: at the University Press, 1930), especially chapters 6 and 10. Paul H. Kocher discusses the relationship between the body and soul in "Body and Soul," in *Science and Religion in Elizabethan England* (San Marino, Calif.: Huntington Library, 1953), chapter 14.

7. *The Complete Poetical Works of Spenser*, ed. R. E. Neil Dodge (Cambridge, Mass.: Riverside Press, 1936), pp. 717–18, 724, 728.

8. Sir Philip Sidney, *Astrophel and Stella*, ed. Max Putzel (Garden City, N.Y.: Doubleday, 1967), pp. 5, 10, 31.

9. In "Justice and Love in *Othello*," *University of Toronto Quarterly* 21 (1952): 330–44, Winifred M. T. Nowottny argues that in Othello's judgment of Cassio, justice and love are compatible values, but in his judgment of Desdemona, justice and love are incompatible, and they become openly conflictive. That is, love for Desdemona invalidates Othello's rational sense of justice.

10. Spenser's females have been discussed elsewhere. Two very different treatments are those by Thomas P. Roche, *The Kindly Flame: A Study of the Third and Fourth Books of Spenser's "Faerie Queene"* (Princeton: Princeton University Press, 1964) and F. M. Padelford, "The Women in Spenser's Allegory of

Love," *Journal of English and Germanic Philology* 16 (1917): 70–
83. Roche studies Britomart, Belphoebe, Amoret, and Florimell, asserting that the relationship of these women and their
stories shapes the intricate structure and meaning of the two
books. Padelford examines Amoret, Belphoebe, Florimell, Radigund, and Britomart in development of his thesis that worthy
love, for Spenser, exists only among those of gentle birth.

11. She is destructive elsewhere, from Book I forward. I
focus on Book VI here because of the paradoxical notion that
man can prove his courtesy by attending to women, yet that
attendance often undercuts the achievement of his quest. One
study of Spenser's destructive women (considering Mirabella,
Paeana, Radigund, Argante, and Acrasia) is J. C. Gray's essay,
"Bondage and Deliverance in the *Faerie Queene*: Varieties of a
Moral Imperative," *Modern Language Review* 70 (1975): 3–12.

12. Humphrey Tonkin, *Spenser's Courteous Pastoral* (Oxford:
Clarendon Press, 1972), p. 31.

13. Kathleen Williams, *Spenser's World of Glass* (Berkeley:
University of California Press, 1966), pp. 196, 202; C. S. Lewis,
The Allegory of Love (New York: Oxford University Press,
1958), p. 351; Tonkin, *Spenser's Courteous Pastoral*, pp. 173–75;
Dorothy Woodward Culp, "Courtesy and Fortune's Chance in
Book VI of the *Faerie Queene*," *Modern Philology* 68 (1972):
254–59. Tonkin sees the sojourn and vision of the Graces as
integral to Calidore's preparation for the defeat of the Beast
(pp. 299–300). Lewis calls the pastoral episode "the core of the
book and the key to Spenser's whole conception of courtesy"
(p. 350). J. C. Maxwell, in "The Truancy of Calidore," *Journal
of English Literary History* 19 (1952): 143–49, sees the episode as
both a truancy and an exemplification of the central virtue of the
book. Maurice Evans, in "Courtesy and the Fall of Man," *English Studies* 46 (1965): 204–20, sees fault in Calidore's behavior
but asserts that Calidore must learn the lesson of courtesy by
rescuing Pastorella.

14. *The Complete Poetical Works of Spenser*, p. 583. Subsequent references will be to this edition and unless otherwise

noted will be to Book VI of *The Faerie Queene*; they will be cited parenthetically by canto and stanza numbers.

15. D. W. Robertson, Jr., *A Preface to Chaucer* (Princeton: Princeton University Press, 1962), pp. 409–10.

16. See discussion cited in note 15. See also Gerald Snare, "The Poetics of Vision: Patterns of Grace and Courtesy in *The Faerie Queene*," *Renaissance Papers* (1974), pp. 1–8. Snare suggests that Calidore's vision of the Graces is abortive because he has forsaken his quest. Paul J. Alpers, in *The Poetry of The Faerie Queene* (Princeton: Princeton University Press, 1967), says that Spenser's admonitions are designed not to permit a decision on the question but rather to make us see the sanctions and motives on both sides (pp. 284–85).

A Concluding
Proposal

The War of the Carrots and the Onions or Concentration versus Dispersion

The Methodology of Interdisciplinary Studies Applied to the European Courts

WILLIAM MELCZER

A poor Renaissance student—as Petrarch used to call himself—is always uneasy and overwhelmed when facing the august originality of the Middle Ages. Compared to a Saint Bonaventure, the portals of Notre Dame la Grande, the steeples of Amiens, Provençal lyrics, and the *Divine Comedy*, what can the Renaissance offer? At the very best, an imitation of classical naturalism. Perhaps, as a consequence of the eternal struggle between succeeding generations, contemporary perspective tries always to cut itself clear from the immediately previous age. That is precisely what happened to Petrarch too. The present may be bad enough, he felt, but the immediate past was much worse. Thus a myth of renewal developed, which is another way of saying that people like to be the generators of their own mistakes rather than the followers of those already tried by others. It is only from a distance that a somewhat more balanced historical perspective emerges. We have needed six hundred years to free ourselves from the bondage of the Petrarchan concept of *renovatio*.

The vast amount of recent Renaissance scholarship, try-

ing hard to carve out a *Lebensraum* for the Renaissance between the towering scholasticism of the Middle Ages and
the acute rationalism of the seventeenth century, did
much, in spite of its avowed aims, to increase our understanding of the Middle Ages themselves. Specifically it
helped to extend continuously its later limits. Dante's
work, which for generations has been considered a sort of
cultural *summa* of the Middle Ages, tends to shift now
from a position of *resumé* to a position of *apogée* and thus
to acquire, much to the chagrin of the poet of the *Canzoniere*, together with, rather than in contradistinction to,
the work of Petrarch, a commanding position of a vast age
that starts with the Carolingians and stretches as far as
Descartes and Galileo, Newton and Vico.

There is the real break. A symptomatic trend in this direction is provided by the many current scholarly colloquia
and learned journals that bear the set of adjectives "Medieval and Renaissance." For quite some time a pervading
feeling has been insinuating itself into the minds of many
of us: the more one studies the Renaissance, the more one
finds oneself in the Middle Ages. In love with Rachel, we
ended up marrying Leah.

Much of the intellectual effort that went into the elucidation of court literature has hitherto remained on more
or less well-traced literary tracks. Except for a few side-
glances at the visual arts and here and there at social and
political history, it is the vertical approach—that is to say,
the understanding of the literary genesis of the works, and
of the transmission of forms, texts, traditions, and motifs, in other words, the literary-poetic structure—that has

held somewhat spellbound the attention of the critics and historians.

Needless to say, such an approach constitutes a legitimate and valid intellectual effort. It is fundamentally a monodisciplinary method that carries all the benefits of a relatively *closed*—I do not say *narrow*—circuit of interests. But such a method carries at the same time all the inherent dangers of a relatively—please, only relatively—closed circuit.

What is the relation of the literary-poetic material to the other artistic, nonliterary forms? More importantly, what is the relation of the literary material to the nonliterary and nonartistic milieu, to the economic, social, and political structure of court life? What is the relation of the literary material to the mentalities, the thinking, the ideologies, and the philosophical-theological thought of its time? And, more precisely, what is the relation of the literary material not so much to court life in general—which is but a thousand-faceted abstraction—but to the life of a particular court at a particular historical moment? Courts, like horses, when seen from afar look all identical. At close range, they are altogether different: one becomes Veillaintif, the other Ipogrifo, the third one Rocinante (I couldn't find a horse in Germany, though I am sure there are many).

Finally there are some still larger queries that time and again pop up, like uncalled and mischievous elves, disturbing the innocent platitudes of our daily pursuits. What is courtly literature? What is courtly love? What is the relation between the two? And what is the relation between courtly literature and the literature of the courts? This seems not an improper distinction to be made. A predominantly, let alone exclusively, literary orientation in the analysis of court literature will be ill at ease in answering some of these questions.

It goes without saying that I do not have the answers to the questions above. But I would like to propose an avenue of research that may open up some possibilities in the future, providing us with a few, of course partial, incomplete, and temporary—alas! like all of our humanistic undertakings—yet, all the same, significant answers to them. The monodisciplinary vertical methodology ought to be complemented with a multidisciplinary horizontal one.

Instead of calling this lecture, insipidly enough, "Concentration versus Dispersion," it occurred to me to call it, lending it a vegetal symbolism so dear to the Middle Ages and reminiscent somewhat of a jolly good Rabelaisian brawl, "The War of the Carrots and the Onions." The worshipers of the carrot are the strict monodisciplinary scholars. Like the carrot, which the more it grows the more it sinks into the earth, so they too dig into the depths of a single hole that constitutes their field of expertise. Busy as they are probing the depth of the hole, the lonely province of their domain, often enough they ignore its location. The worshipers of the onion, on the other hand, are the strictly multidisciplinary scholars. Like the rings of the onion, they spread themselves thin over a large number of fields, without breaking the ground in any. Knowing the location of all, they are at home in none.

Between carrots and onions, I opt for a salad of both. Between secluded and narrow monodisciplinarism and dilettantish and superficial multidisciplinarism, I propose, for the study of the European courts, an interdisciplinary approach, a veritable dialogue of the disciplines, somewhat in the manner of the dialogue of the sister arts. Such an interdisciplinary dialogue, far from invalidating the findings of the single disciplines involved, will coordinate and integrate the bewildering complexity of the multifarious trends of the single-track research efforts. But for the particular task we have in mind, the study of European court literature, a further convergence seems imperative. In order to establish the historic coordinates of the literature of the courts, as well as of the court itself, we must first establish those coordinates for a *particular* court at a *particular* time.

The convergence is thus a double one: in terms of the objectives of the research; and in terms of the intellectual tools with which we attack them. In other words it is team work, *un travail d'équipe*, we are advocating. As in scientific operations complex research laboratories are set up with dozens, often hundreds, of researchers in order to grapple with a particular problem, so we too must constitute ourselves into larger research units, formulate mutually agreeable goals, and collaborate in the solution of well-defined though complex problems. Otherwise many of our research efforts, brilliant as these may be, will fall upon deaf ears and much of their valuable impact will waste away.

What in our case do we mean by "un travail d'équipe"? A certain court is singled out, within certain well-defined and historically significant time limits. For instance, the court of Alfonso el Sabio, or the court of Frederick II in

Foggia, or the court of Saint Louis, or that of Jean le Bon up to Maupertuis. Allowance is made for diachronic and diagraphic developments: the *Wanderlust*, often a euphemism for *Wandernot*, of many of our medieval poets is proverbial. Courts themselves, especially in the earlier periods, were often on the move, planting their banner now here, now there. With all these elements in mind a research objective is thus defined.

Next, research teams are set up in as many relevant disciplines as it is deemed necessary—economics, social history, political history, ecclesiastical history, the history of images, imaginative literature, architecture, town planning, musicology, the history of spectacles, and so on. If a field proves to be too complex, it is subdivided; if it looks poor, it is eliminated. Common sense, as always, remains an important operative ingredient.

By concentrating its study on the designated objective, each team of researchers comes up, within say a year or two, with a set of findings, which are then presented in a conference discussion forum with the other disciplines present.

Voilà. That's all. The dialogue of the disciplines.

Objection: Sometimes the reports will fall upon deaf ears.

Answer: True. Scholars like to talk rather than to listen. But that is what happens in monodisciplinary ventures too.

Objection: Too complicated. Too many teams and too many people involved.

Answer: Not really. Six or seven teams, each of them with four or five, or perhaps more, researchers, make about thirty or forty people working on a single court-period. It is a jolly good group.

Objection: Members of a team, working laboriously toward a conference, are located in distant places, often in far-off countries. Communication and coordination problems are likely to arise.

Answer: Old-fashioned epistolary correspondence.

Objection: The *letterato* knows but little about iconography, which is the province of the art historian; and the art historian knows but little about archives and state documents, which are the province of the political historian. None of the three knows anything about town planning or architecture.

Answer: That is *good*: "les mariages inégaux font des beaux enfants." They may know little about each other's discipline, but they are talking about essentially the same historicocultural entity. Hence, associations, parallels, contrasts, which otherwise might have remained undetected, will now become apparent. An unexpected sidelight cast from a foreign discipline often illuminates one's own. Furthermore it is easier to take criticism from the neighbor, and we all know the old saying that the prophet is not heeded in his own land.

Objection: Since each discipline has its own lingo, what its practitioners call learnedly *termini tecnici*, in the heat of the debate some misunderstandings and even some roughness may be expected.

Answer: That is *very good*. Firstly, it will teach each discipline that what they have been tacitly and for so long taking for granted holds but a relative certainty, often shaky at its very foundation. Secondly, it will teach that the idiosyncratic terminology of each discipline is nothing but a security blanket. Helpful at home, it is useless abroad. Trying to explain the terminology to the noninitiated is the best way to clarify its meaning for its practitioner. We must certainly be familiar with this didactic rule of thumb, for it constitutes nothing else but the very essence of our teaching. Thirdly, roughness in the debate is what logicians call Hegelian dialectical progression.

Question: Which court to choose?

Answer: Not too small a one, to have enough material to work with; and not too large a one, to make the research manageable. A modest court will do. From the distance, any small court will look quite innocent (who knows much of the court of Bamberg under the Princely Bishop Heinrich von Schmiedefeld?). At a close range, though, they are all fearfully and forbiddingly complex. Hence the motto: a little bit less will be a little bit more.

Question: If half a dozen of us work on one court, what will the rest of us do? May we initiate research on a second court?

Answer: What will you do? What you have always been doing. Otherwise, you may initiate as many new projects as you wish. But I would observe a controlled moderation.

Question: And what then, after the conference, the discussion, and the exchange of ideas?

Answer: The studies are published. For instance: *Court of Jean le Bon, Phase 1*. Then everybody goes home and continues the intellectual labor leading to the *Court of Jean le Bon, Phase 2, e così via*. Positive integers are infinite. So are humanistic studies. They have only a beginning, no end.

Question: Who pays for the conference, the publication, the research?

Answer: I do not know.

Question: *A quoi bon tout ça?*

To this the answer must be somewhat longer. In the course of such concentrated interdisciplinary research it will become apparent that there is not a one-to-one relationship between the economic, sociopolitical, and ideological forces operative in a determined court and their literary and cultural expression. Literature is the indirect, often imperfect, and always kaleidoscopic reflection of an underlying reality, be that reality aristocratic, bourgeois, ecclesiastic, or a combination of all or some of these. For the late medieval and the early Renaissance courts it now seems that that reality was somewhat less aristocratic, certainly less exclusively aristocratic, than is commonly believed. At the same time, and parallel to the kaleidoscopic image literature projects, that very literature becomes part and parcel of the reality it so imperfectly reflects.

In concrete terms, the benefits we may expect from an interdisciplinary, centripetal study of one European court, or of a number of European courts, are the following:

a. We will be in a more advantageous position to establish the cross-cultural influences between the old burg and the new burg, between the *castellani* or *castrenses* and the *cives* or burghers. We will learn that the literature and other artistic expressions of the courts and of the rising bourgeois culture are less than hermetically separated from each other.

b. We will be able to ascertain the idiosyncratic features and the *sui generis* development of each court period we undertake to study by establishing in each case a set of economic, social, political, and cultural coordinates. The gradual definition of single court periods will lead us to a gradual definition of the court itself, as a historically conditioned changing global phenomenon.

c. We will be able to understand better the cultural implications of court life by studying simultaneously the social and economic conditions out of which they were born and to which they were born and to which they are intrinsically related.

d. Finally, we will be in a somewhat better position to define the vexing questions of what is courtly literature and what is literature of the courts.

The road to be traveled is long and not an easy one. But there are no shortcuts in such undertakings.

More importantly perhaps, the prospect attained at the end of the journey—not really the end, but any place we may stop awhile for a little rest—may result in some uneasiness to more than one of us. Something of the mystic glamour attached to the late medieval and early Renaissance aristocratic court will vanish in the process. The prince will lose some stature; the princess, chastity; paramours, their golden tresses; and from the back yard of the aristocratic court some uneasy voices will rise. Even more weightily, the ascending urban bourgeoisie, thriving on an early capitalist economy, will increasingly incorporate, in the measure of its ability to allocate purchasing power, the artistic and literary privileges (and also tastes) of the court.

To those who like to cling to the romantic image of the Middle Ages, little consolation can I offer except this: the acquisition of historical knowledge occurs always at the expense of historical myth. And to those who are little impressed by such a positivistic assertion, I can offer yet another, if you allow, a Christian consolation: the deglorification of mankind or of any segment thereof only brings us near to the proto-image of man, to the Christ image incarnated in each of us. A sublime simplicity emerges once the superfluous paraphernalia is shed off. Who exemplifies such a sublime simplicity better than Dante?

> Ma quell' altro magnanimo, a cui posta
> restato m'era, non mutò aspetto,
> né mosse collo, né piegò sua costa★
> [*Inf.* x.73–75]

Much of what comes into our hands as the choicest specimen of courtly literature constitutes, in economic terms, the cultural fringe benefits of a salary earned in hard currency. A few examples will do to illustrate such a realistic hard line.

The late eleventh and the twelfth centuries witnessed the economic resurgence of urban civilization. The cities, and with them early bourgeois capitalism, were in the making. A corps of professional administrators, the distant ancestors of today's meticulously efficient French *fonctionnaires*, put itself to the service of the newly generated centralized urban power. The paradigmatic consequences of this new economic and geopolitical situation are apparent in the administratively most advanced country of the late twelfth and early thirteenth centuries in Europe: the Norman kingdom of Sicily.

★But the other, that great soul at whose instance I had stopped, changed not his aspect, nor moved his neck, nor bent his side.

In administrative no less than in other matters, Roger's court in Palermo did not have to start from scratch. His administration had inherited a sophisticated Byzantine tradition. Many of his officers were of Greek or Arab extraction. The accounts of the royal treasury were kept by Arab scribes better versed in mathematical science than most of their western colleagues. Roger's court was cosmopolitan, enlightened, and magnificent. The Pantocrator in Cefalù is Byzantine, but the legends of the stupendous mosaics are in Latin. Similarly, the largest-ever Christian iconographic program in Monreale glitters in stately Byzantine magnificence, while the main bronze door of the same cathedral executed by Bonannus da Pisa is already Romanesque, and its *legenda* constitutes one of the earliest specimens of a Latin in the very process of transmuting into Italo-Tuscan.

When Frederick II, in his turn, outgrew the tutelage of Innocent III, he found a ready-made foundation for an empire. Crowned successively in Aachen, Rome, and Jerusalem—the latter, a self-coronation, but that mattered little; was not Petrarch's also a carefully engineered self-coronation?—Frederick set up his court, unassumingly, in Foggia. It is from there—not for nothing did he always consider himself *puer Apuliae*—and not from Palermo that the new rationalism, secularization, and pre-Renaissance classicism shone with unusual brilliance. The *Liber Augustalis*, the *delicato parlare*, the philosophical exchanges with Arab and Jewish scholars, the *De arte venandi cum avibus*, and the *Scuola siciliana* are only a few of the cultural achievements of this wonder of the world. At the same time, however, Frederick knew how to deal with the less-

than-dignified tasks of his office. Assisted by Pier delle
Vigne, the Chancellor whom we find in Dante's *Inferno*
uncomfortably imprisoned in a thorn-tree, Frederick centralized the minting rights, kept an army of slaves, wild
beasts, and mistresses—in this order—and dealt variously, but always effectively, with those who charged him,
rightly so it seems, with atheism, heresy, despotism, and
concupiscence.

Frederick was not alone in his minting preoccupations.
When Filarete, much later, lays out in his *Trattato d'archi-
tettura* the central square of a city-court, he makes sure that
the mint is a stone's throw from the princely palace:

At the eastern end I will build the cathedral, and the royal court
at the western. . . . In the northern part of the piazza I will make
the merchant's piazza, . . . On the southern side of the piazza I
will make another piazza that will be a sort of market where
edibles can be sold, for example meat, fruit, vegetables, and
other things necessary to the life of man. . . . At the head I will
make the Palazzo del Capitano on the corner nearest the court,
so that only the street separates them. In the merchant's market
I will make, on one end, the Palazzo del Podestà and opposite
it the law courts. On the northern part I will make the munici-
pal prison. This will be directly behind the law courts. On the
eastern part, at the corner of the piazza, I will make the mint,
where money is made and stored, and near it the customshouse.[1]

Having determined the location of the mint in the plani-
fication of the town, Filarete feels that the rest can indeed
wait.

An utterly unromantic picture emerges: power, food,
and other pleasures, all of which are kept in balance and
tied together by the string of the purse. It is a hymn of
praise to the Carolingian monetary reform introduced by

Charlemagne: the stability of society is measured, rather than in terms of chivalric honor, in terms of the stability of its currency.

Much before Colbert and Richelieu, late medieval German proverbs already teach us that "Geld behält das Feld" (Money is master of the field) and that "Wo Geld ist will Geld hin" (Where money is, money goes), which later on was euphemistically converted into "Wo die Tauben sind, fliegen die Tauben zu" (Where the doves are, there the doves fly to). Remembering Dante's sublime

> Quali colombi dal disio chiamate
> con l'ali alzate e ferme al dolce nido
> vegnon per l'aere, dal voler portate . . ..†
>   [*Inf.* v.82–84]

one cannot help feeling an unglorious chill.

When Gucciardini, that modern historian of the early sixteenth century, compares Lorenzo de' Medici and Cosimo, the *Pater Patriae*, he pays little attention to Lorenzo's garden museum, his painfully assembled collection of codices, his lavish patronage of Leonardo, Michelangelo, Ficino, and Poliziano, let alone Lorenzo's own *Canti Carnascialeschi* or *Canti Spirituali*. What really interests him is which of the two men did more to enrich the coffers of the state as well as those of his own. Of the two, Cosimo is found by far the better man, because "although he had many cares of state, he did not neglect commerce and his private affairs; rather he managed them with so much diligence and skill that his wealth was always greater than the

---

† As doves called by desire, with wings raised and steady, come through the air, borne by their will to their sweet nest . . ..

state's, which was enormous."² Against this, Lorenzo receives but a poor review: "In private affairs and commerce he had very little aptitude, so that when they went badly, he was forced to use public money and on occasions probably also other people's private fortunes, which brought him considerable reproach and blame" (pp. 9–10). As Gucciardini concludes, Lorenzo was no great builder of walls. Instead of the refinements of the court, we are back where we were two thousand years earlier, at the time of the *Urbs condita*.

Such documents, taken from the economic, social, and political history, and the history of mentalities—call them documents of life, if you wish—are variously integrated into the frame of reference of the magnate, the prince, the duke, the king, in one word, of courtly power. It is to similar documents that the literature of the courts must also be integrated. We might do well to remember Jean Meschinot's grim lines:

> La court est une mer dont sourt
> Vagues d'orgueil, d'envie orage:
> . . . Ire esmeut debas et oultrage
> Qui les nefs gittent souvent bas,
> Traison y fait son personnage.‡³

There should be no illusion. That is the court. Or, at least, that is *also* the court.

Et d'ici, où est-ce qu'on va?

To art. To courtly literature and to the literature of the

---

‡The court is a sea from which arise / Waves of pride, a storm of envy: / . . . Wrath causes strife and excesses / Which often destroy ships, / Treason plays his role.

courts as art. To art as a restorer of balance. To art as a redeeming force in life. To art as both vaccine and antidote.

That is the reason why I have promised you that, at the end of the disciplines, the literature of the courts will emerge in a stronger and manlier light than before. The literature of the courts will emerge in a stronger and manlier light because the quality of its intrinsic beauty is now found projected against a rich, polyphonic, often contrasting and bewildering background. The many-sided ripeness of life is only beneficial to art.

And now one more word on courtly literature.

Since we all know the tautology "a rose is a rose is a rose is a rose," we all try to avoid it. But then, at times, unawares, because usually we work in closed circuits without some handy extradisciplinary control, and because regarding courtly literature, the literature of the courts, courtly love, and the court we generalize too much and particularize too little, we tend to make inferences and fall into a misleading paratautology. Instance 1: courtly literature and the literature of the courts are two distinct things. While all courtly literature pertains to the literature of the courts, not all literature of the courts pertains to courtly literature. Instance 2: since courtly love is often found in courtly literature, and courtly literature is supposed to reflect the life of the court, court life is often identified with courtly love. Instance 3: one talks of *the court*, while one ought to talk about *the courts*. These are, admittedly, gross examples; but a residual element of this paratautology is around us.

The cult of women blended with the traditional cult of

military prowess to form a kind of secular religion, a courtly pseudo-ethos, aristocratic and sophisticated, that planted its banner in the castles of the nobility first, and in the urban palaces later. When Andreas Capellanus describes in chapter 4 of his *De amore* the persons that are fit for love, he mentions, in one and the same breath, arms and love. Everlasting bonfires did not deter the pious nobility from emulating, at least *in spirito*, Aucassin, who would rather follow all the sweet ladies and goodly knights to hell than go to heaven without them.

When in Italy the nobility made the cities their place of residence—*ubi bene, ibi patria*—they continued to cling to the courtly *devotio*. Sweet was this *devotio profana*. Sweet and tenacious. So sweet indeed that Boiardo, writing at the court of the Estes in Ferrara at the end of the fifteenth century, still speaks of the same sweet ladies and goodly knights; and Ariosto, a little later, opens the very best seller of the Renaissance with

> Le donne, i cavalier, l'arme, gli amori,
> Le courtesie, le audaci imprese io canto.★4

In a chiastic structure that made history, women and love encompass and sustain knights and arms, and deeds of courtesy precede those of war.

By then half a millennium had elapsed since courtly literature first made its appearance on the European scene. What seems so remarkable is not the fact that the quality of the courtly spirit had changed radically during that

★The ladies, the knights, the arms, the loves, the courtesies, the bold exploits I sing.

time, but the concomitant fact that, in one way or another, in diachronic and diagraphic developments, the courtly spirit had indeed lasted so long.

Who will be the last of the knights still indulging in courtly love? Who else but the "Caballero de la triste figura" whom Cervantes gently and unheroically lays to rest in his bed. "'Ah, master,' cried Sancho through his tears, 'don't die, your Grace, but take my advice and go on living for many years to come. . . . Look you, don't be lazy but get up from this bed and let us go out into the fields clad as shepherds as we agreed to do. Who knows but behind some bush we may come upon the lady Dulcinea, as disenchanted as you could wish.'"[5] But Don Quixote is not in a mood to start again. From Neoplatonic euphoria he has fallen into Aristotelian melancholia. That is his end. And that is the end, on a European scale, of courtly literature too. It is King Arthur who dies in Don Quixote. Would it not be more appropriate to say that with him the Middle Ages is laid to rest?

The less-than-glorious image of the European courts of the Middle Ages and of the Renaissance that may emerge from our interdisciplinary undertaking should not deflect our determination to proceed on the road of historical veracity. As the art of courtly love has been transmuted into the art of courtly literature, so now the art of courtly literature must generate the art of critique of European court culture.

An old Viennese anecdote tells us that the shaky generals of the Austro-Hungarian empire (what Stefan Zweig called *Die Welt von Gestern*) were but in one respect better off than their military colleagues abroad: it was in their capacity for laughter. They could, in fact, laugh three times at each joke. They laughed at it for the first time when they were told the joke. They laughed at it for the second time when the joke was explained to them. And they laughed at it for the third time when they finally understood the joke.

Mutatis mutandis, so it fares with us too, or it may fare with us too, when facing the literature of the courts. First we appreciate, cherish, and enjoy it when, unhampered by intellectual sophistication (isn't that a glorious approach?), we find ourselves in a nonmediate contact with the literary-poetic material. Second, we appreciate, cherish, and enjoy it when, applying the literary-historical-critical tools at our disposal, we dissect that piece of literature in order to recompose it in aesthetically and literarily meaningful patterns. And third, we appreciate, cherish, and enjoy it when we approach the cultural phenomenon of the literature of the courts from a wider, more generous, interdisciplinary perspective.

The interdisciplinary methodology for the study of the European courts is neither a Curtana able to cut through all maze and thicket, nor a panacea able to cure all ills. It is simply, and modestly—*comme il le faut*—one more avenue of research. It is an avenue not supplanting, but complementing, the vertical disciplinary research. In humanistic studies there are no final questions as there are no final answers. There are only reinterpretations. That is one of the few consolations we have when comparing the sorry state of our profession with the greener pastures of science, social science, and technology. In the humanities, alas, nothing becomes obsolete, because nothing is completely novel, and because ideas have an intrinsic historic value. While scientific libraries are small and neat, humanistic libraries grow as the dust grows. We all may end up one day in that museum of ideas.

But with these inherent limitations, the interdisciplinary methodology offered here has the capability of providing some historically conditioned answers to this sometimes mysterious and fascinating, often elusive and imponderable, but always enchanting and beautiful literature of the courts.

I have taken too much of your time, and I have taxed your patience even more. I must ask for your forgiveness. My defense is an old one, used at banquet tables since times immemorial. So long as there is food on the table, we are bound to eat. And the banquet tables at Prospero's island have just now vanished. Having thus consumed our frugal dish of carrots and onions, we too may now go.

NOTES

1. Filarete, *Treatise on Architecture*, trans. John R. Spencer (New Haven: Yale University Press, 1965), 1:74.

2. Guicciardini, *History of Italy and History of Florence*, trans. Cecil Grayson (New York: Washington Square Press, 1964), p. 9.

3. Pierre Champion, *Histoire poétique du quinzième siècle* (Paris: Edouard Champion, 1923), 2:219.

4. Ludovico Ariosto, *Orlando Furioso* (Milan: Ulrico Hoepli, 1973), p. 1.

5. Miguel de Cervantes, *The Ingenious Gentleman Don Quixote de la Mancha*, trans. Samuel Putnam (New York: Viking Press, 1949), p. 986.

The Contributors
and
Index

Notes on Contributors

JOHN M. BOWERS teaches English at the University of Virginia in Charlottesville and recently spent three years as a Rhodes Scholar at Merton College, Oxford.

MATILDA TOMARYN BRUCKNER teaches French at Princeton University, has published in *Studies in Medieval Culture*, and is looking forward to publication of her monograph dealing with narrative invention in the twelfth century as seen in the hospitality convention.

WILLIAM CALIN is professor and head of the Department of Romance Languages at the University of Oregon. Among his many works that would interest readers of this volume are *The Old French Epic of Revolt*, *The Epic Quest*, *A Poet at the Fountain*, and *Crown, Cross and Fleur-de-lis*.

LOWANNE E. JONES, assistant director of the Center for Medieval Studies at Ohio State University, has recently published *The 'Cort d'Amor': A Thirteenth-Century Allegorical Art of Love*.

WINIFRED GLEASON KEANEY teaches English at George Mason University in Fairfax, Virginia. She is working on a critical edition and study of the prose style of Sir John Fortescue's *The Governance of England (1471–1476)*.

DONALD MADDOX is Andrew Mellon Scholar in Medieval Studies (1976–79) at Brandeis University. His works include *Structure and Sacring: The Systematic Kingdom in Chrétien's "Erec,"* and he coedits *Degré Second*, a new French literary journal.

WILLIAM MELCZER is professor of Comparative Literature and History of Ideas of the Renaissance at Syracuse University. He is also an honorary president of the ICLS. His numerous publications on humanism, the history of thought in the Middle Ages and the Renaissance, and literature, link the cultures of Italy, Spain, France, England, and the Low Countries to the continuity of classical learning in the West.

FLORENCE H. RIDLEY, professor of English at UCLA, specializes in Chaucer and the Scots Chaucerians. Among her publications are *The Prioress and the Critics* and *Middle Scots Poetry: A Checklist*.

TERENCE SCULLY teaches medieval French language and literature at Wilfrid Laurier University in Waterloo, Ontario. He has studied, in particular, courtly love in the fourteenth century, has published Mahieu le Poirier's *Le Court d'Amours*, and is at work editing the texts of all fourteenth-century French polyphonic songs.

NATHANIEL SMITH, secretary-treasurer of the ICLS, teaches in the Department of Modern Foreign Languages and Literatures at Boston University. He has published *Figures of Repetition in the Old Provençal Lyric: A Study in the Style of the Troubadours* and collaborated in the second edition of Hill and Bergin, *Anthology of the Provençal Troubadours.*

JOSEPH SNOW teaches Spanish and Portuguese at the University of Georgia. He has written annotated bibliographies of studies of the poetry of Alfonso X of Castile and of the Spanish masterwork *La Celestina.* He also edits an international newsletter *Celestinesca.* His current project is a book highlighting the *Cantigas de Santa Maria* as a transition between the troubadours and the fourteenth- and fifteenth-century Spanish *cancioneros.*

SARA STURM-MADDOX is professor of French and Italian at the University of Massachusetts at Amherst. She has published *The Lay of Guingamor: A Study*, *Lorenzo de' Medici*, and various articles on medieval French, Italian, and Spanish literature. Her current project is a booklength study of Petrarch's *Canzoniere.*

The late EUGÈNE VINAVER was a leading expert on Malory and medieval romance. He was emeritus professor at Manchester University and had been a visiting professor at several North American universities. Among his many important works are his editions of Malory's tales of King Arthur, his *A la recherche d'une poétique médiévale*, and *The Rise of Romance.*

FRIEDERIKE WIESMANN-WIEDEMANN, who teaches at Northeastern Illinois University, is the author of *Le Roman du "Willehalm" de Wolfram d'Eschenbach et l'Epopée d'"Aliscans": Étude de la transformation de l'epopée en roman.*

Index